BEARS IN THE BIRD FEEDERS

BEARS
IN THE
BIRD FEEDERS

COTTAGE LIFE ON SHAMAN'S ROCK

Jim Poling, Sr.

DUNDURN
TORONTO

Editor: Jennifer McKnight
Design: Jesse Hooper
Printer: Webcom

Library and Archives Canada Cataloguing in Publication

Poling, Jim (Jim R.)

    Bears in the bird feeders : cottage life on Shaman's Rock / Jim Poling.

Includes bibliographical references and index.
Issued also in electronic format.
ISBN 978-1-4597-0218-9

    1. Vacation homes--Ontario. 2. Country life--Ontario.
I. Title.

GV191.6.P65 2013   643.25   C2012-903196-8

1 2 3 4 5   17 16 15 14 13

We acknowledge the support of the **Canada Council for the Arts** and the **Ontario Arts Council** for our publishing program. We also acknowledge the financial support of the **Government of Canada** through the **Canada Book Fund** and **Livres Canada Books**, and the **Government of Ontario** through the **Ontario Book Publishing Tax Credit** and the **Ontario Media Development Corporation**.

Care has been taken to trace the ownership of copyright material used in this book. The author and the publisher welcome any information enabling them to rectify any references or credits in subsequent editions.

J. Kirk Howard, President

Printed and bound in Canada.

VISIT US AT
Dundurn.com | Definingcanada.ca | @dundurnpress | Facebook.com/dundurnpress

Dundurn	Gazelle Book Services Limited	Dundurn
3 Church Street, Suite 500	White Cross Mills	2250 Military Road
Toronto, Ontario, Canada	High Town, Lancaster, England	Tonawanda, NY
M5E 1M2	L41 4XS	U.S.A. 14150

To Diane, the rock on which all this is built

TABLE OF CONTENTS

ACKNOWLEDGEMENTS

Despite all our electronic tools and gadgetry, people still are the most important resource in making a book. These are some of the people who helped make *Birds in the Bird Feeders* a reality:

Stuart Robertson, friend and lawyer, whose passion for good stories well told provided much valued advice and criticism, as he did for another important story, *Waking Nanabijou.*

Penny Caldwell, editor of *Cottage Life*, who took time to read the manuscript for me, and who in the past has made writing for the magazine so much fun.

Ellen Wiley of Coldwell Banker Wiley Real Estate in Dorset for her insights into cottage properties and cottage country.

David Currie, a Huntsville lawyer, who was kind enough to give me a good briefing on road allowances and other cottage legalities.

Brad Robinson of Robinson's General Store in Dorset, whose deep knowledge really qualifies him as Mr. Cottage Country.

Lorne Heise, who told me all about cottage water systems and whose invention rescued me from Screaming Saturdays.

And two people who do artwork for fun and relaxation: My aunt Zita Poling Moynan of Sault Ste. Marie and my son Jim Poling of Hamilton, who I always knew could write, but who surprised me with his wonderful outdoor painted scenes.

INTRODUCTION

G oing to the cottage is like going to school. You learn all kinds of stuff. For instance, mosquitoes start having sex when they are two days old. And blackflies do not pollinate blueberry bushes. There are new lessons every day at the cottage; lessons on how to live as a part of nature, without always trying to dominate it.

This is a book of observations and reflections on those snatches of life lived away from the wired, frenetic life of an urban society that is driving more and more people nuts. (A study published in the June 2011 issue of *Nature* found that schizophrenia is twice as high for people born and raised in cities.) It follows cottage life through the four seasons, reminding us that clocks, land deeds, and even the set dates for seasons are human inventions with little meaning in nature.

In school we learned that solstices mark the beginnings of winter and summer. Equinoxes start spring and fall. All four are marked on calendars, roughly on the twenty-first day of every third month starting in March. Interesting, but none of that matters at the cottage. The dates are arbitrary and artificial; just names based on mathematical calculations made by humans. Ask the locals when spring will arrive and they will tell you: "The snow comes in its own good time, and the snow goes in its own good time."

Exactly. Seasons change when they are ready to change. Spring begins when snow and ice locking lakes and land melt and break up. Fall starts when chlorophyll in the leaves diminishes, causing green leaves to take on brilliant anthocyanin pigments. Winter really starts when Manidoo-Giizisoons, the Ojibwe Little Spirit moon, appears in December.

Cottage country people don't see spring's arrival on the calendar, or the television news. They feel the change of the seasons on their faces, hear it in the trees, smell it in the air. That's why cottagers act differently, think differently, and generally live differently at the cottage. That's why many of us take off our watches at the cottage, or the cabin, camp, lake house, or whatever you call it in your part of the world. (In my part of the world it's cottage, but in Northern Ontario it's camp, while in much of the United States it's the cabin, and in other places the chalet.) Exact times do not matter, except perhaps for those awful moments when it's time to leave.

This book reflects on how to get along with the wilder cottage neighbours: the bears, coyotes, and smaller critters that have little respect for cottagers' stuff. It also includes observations on getting along with governments, especially in the area of building codes and land use. It observes how governments, with their unquenchable thirst for revenue, too often forget the heritage and history so important in helping us to remember the traditions and values that helped carve this country from wilderness. And how politics and lack of vision shutter places such as Ontario's Leslie Frost Centre, which once gave nature-deficient urban kids an opportunity to see, hear, and feel the natural world, and understand that we are part of the wildness of it.

Cottagers understand how things might go easier for humankind if more issues were examined around campfires, in a softer, reflective light and without heated debate. People gathered at campfires, perhaps soothed by the tranquility, tend to listen and think more clearly before they speak. We all should live a bit more naturally and easier, giving more thoughtful reflection to the many problems that face us.

Cottage life is changing. In North America, cottages used to be unheated cabins of two-by-four wall construction intended for use in the summer months only. Building rules and regulations demanded more elaborate structures, which were made possible by new building materials. Society became more affluent and it made economic sense to build a place that could be used in all seasons.

Cottages have never been just for the rich, however. What makes cottages so special is that many of them belong to average folks who were willing to give up weekends and holidays to saw boards, hammer nails, and push rocks around to create their dream place outside the city.

Another change in cottage country is the arrival of people whose recent roots were in other countries. More and more of what used to be visible minorities are seen in cottage country. And, that is good because it is important for all Canadians, most of who now live in urban settings, to be in touch with the outdoor spirit that built this country.

BREAKUP

— 1 —
AWAKENING

"Nature does not hurry, yet everything is accomplished."
— LAO TZU

*P*link.
The first one is indistinguishable. Perhaps imagined, not really heard. Then I hear it again. *Plink. Plink.*

I tentatively slide back the silky, warm duvet that hides my head on bitter cottage mornings. The cold air pressing down on the covers shocks me into wanting to burrow deeper, but I listen instead. *Plink, plink. Plink, plink.*

It is not imagined. It is a sound, increasingly real as *plink, plink, plink* becomes a persistent beat, then a patter. It is the sound of water dripping from the metal roof sweating snow in the early morning sun. The drips are steady and strong enough that my mind's eye sees them boring through the snowdrift on the deck until they are thumping the wood with splattering thuds.

This is the first signal that the bullying winter is backing off, however grudgingly. It is winter's first backward step in a retreat that begins with a single *plink*, and ends with the last patch of grey ice giving way to myriad sunbeams frolicking on open water.

It is the first sound of the Great Transformation; the sound of hope, warmth, brightness, freshness, and the cottage freedom that spring brings. It fills me with anticipation, almost enough to think about abandoning the warm bed, but not quite. So I lie there, savouring the sound and reflecting on all that it means.

I am one of the luckiest cottagers because I get to use the cottage all year round. Our numbers have grown over the last ten years because of work flex hours, the wired society, and the fact that cottages are now too major an investment just to be used during the skinny summer season.

Shaman's Rock, which I named my lake paradise when I fell in love with it a lifetime ago, favours the morning sun. The spring sun embraces the broad metal roof facing south and peers into the windows to warm the pine woodwork, armchairs, and leather couch. This natural solar heating comes at no cost, so I let it do its job before I slip from bed and onto the chilly floor.

Spring's first kiss creates a major shift in cottage life, from survival mode to action mode. Cottage country can move ahead now into all those projects suspended late last fall when the water stiffened, and everything but the biggest buildings and bare trees disappeared beneath relentless snow squalls.

The cottagers who battened their places down and fled for the winter can start thinking about their return. For those of us who make regular winter visits there is more to think about now than simply wood for heat and keeping open the pathways to the outside world. There are new chores to be done, new projects to organize. Many new things to experience and to learn.

Cottaging is all about experiences and learning. It is a form of higher education. Like university, it is much hard work mixed with much fun, and new lessons come every day, no matter how many years of learning you already have. The winter just ending, for instance, has reprised the lesson that a lone human with a shovel and an axe is a poor match for a cottage world that becomes shrink wrapped as the snow builds. The dripping of the water from the roof means the shrinking is done, and the outside world is expanding, setting free all denizens of the forest and the lakeside cabins.

What eventually dumps me from bed is the acceptance that no matter how early or how extended the spring, time for the cottager is limited. Much snow remains and below-freezing temperatures persist, but in fewer than sixty days, the *plink* of roof runoff will be replaced by the droning of myriad little creatures that bite and sting. They'll be here by mid-May just as sure as God gave humans networks of blood vessels already pulsating in the dreams of a trillion bugs, now sleeping as mere embryos. Mosquitoes, blackflies, gnats, no-see-ums, and anything else that flies and cherishes the succulence of fresh blood in the northern woods. When they come, the outside spring chores had better be done.

Still, there is no need for getting crazy and rushing outside. Beyond the bedcovers are an armchair, warm fire, hot coffee, and some quiet reflection, all important stages in preparing to venture out. Besides, snow melting off the roof does not a winter's end make. There is a snow storm or two yet to come, certainly in April and maybe even May, but their punches will be pulled.

The cottage veteran measures winter's death throes by leaving the armchair, pouring another cup of coffee, and staring out a window. Nature provides the black and white rule, an accurate measuring system for deciding when to go out. When you stare out into the back hillsides and see nothing but white you have 100 percent winter. When small black patches of rock outcroppings appear, and dark shadows show at the bases of the oaks and maples, that's about 10 percent spring, 90 percent winter. When the black to white ratio reaches about 65 to 35, it's safe to go out without snowshoes.

There's no use getting wound tight about when that will happen. As the locals say, the snow comes on its own and leaves on its own.

When the time arrives, walking the perimeters of the receding snow is joyous freedom. I feel like Julie Andrews frolicking through an alpine meadow singing "The hills are alive...." Ecstasy is stepping on pieces of turf not seen for five months.

The dying snows have left behind white gossamer mildew, sandy grit, and the bones of rotting oak leaves, but the spring rains soon will wash that away. Nature is good at cleaning itself up. What it can't clean up and heal are the winter wounds inflicted on the cottager's stuff, the buildings, docks, decks, and outdoor toys.

The wounds of the past winter fortunately are only superficial. A broken eavestrough and some downed branches. Not like the savage winter of 2008–09 when thick ice build-up grabbed the bathroom vent stack, ripped it free, and left a hole in the cottage roof. One end of a steel snow guard was twisted like a pretzel. Ice crashing off the roof knocked the barbecue for a double loop. The pipe framing on the storage tent up the hill was left sagging despite the reinforcement added the previous fall.

The power of ice is awesome. How can light, fluffy flakes, even tens of millions of them, transform into concrete-like masses of such weight and brute strength? When ice creeps, as a glacier or seemingly harmless rooftop sheet, it grinds, chews, rips, and tears anything in its path, including finger-length screw nails securing the snow guards.

Roof snow deepens and gains weight without anyone noticing. One weekend it's a few centimetres, a couple of weekends later it is twenty or more. Anyone who ventures up on the roof later in the winter usually is shocked to find that the apparent twenty centimetres of snow seen from ground actually is about one metre. Sun and moisture harden the snow, and heat inside the cottage radiates through the roof and turns the first layers of snow to ice. Dealing with the ice creates one of the cottager's many dilemmas: should the cottage have a steel roof or shingled roof?

Photograph by the author.

Cottagers' dilemma: Steel roof or shingled roof? A steel roof lasts longer than shingles but releases heavy loads of ice and snow. You don't want to be under this load when it lets go.

Steel lasts longer and allows snow masses to slide off during any of winter's milder moments. But anything below the roof's edge — deck railings, left out furniture, barbeques, small dogs, and people — is doomed when the weighty masses of snow and ice roll, take flight, and crash down.

A new metal roof for Shaman's Rock seemed like a good idea a few years back. We quickly learned, however, that our new roof released its snow and ice at the main front entrance and along the side deck. Anyone going in or out of the place when the roof let go its load could be seriously injured or killed. So we installed snow and ice barriers to stop dangerous slides.

The first guards were those plastic retainers about the size of a small adult hand. They are screw-nailed at strategic spots along the roof to hold the snow and ice from sliding. I might as well have put Pringles potato chips up there. Most of them snapped or were uprooted, screws and all, during their first winter.

Then we went to heavy angle iron steel guards. They seemed to be the solution to sudden, dangerous ice slides. They just slowed the roof snow pack, allowing it to form little glaciers that were sometimes strong enough to rip the guards from their roof mounts. I was wishing we had stayed with the old-fashioned asphalt shingles. We changed because shingles have a shorter life than a steel roof and are less durable. Also, I tired of the mid-winter roof shovelling and the spring cleanout of shingle grit in the eavestroughs.

An asphalt shingle roof has its own disadvantages. Snow and ice bond to the shingles and stay there all winter, building tons of weight. Building codes specify how cottage roofs must be built to bear huge snow loads. Time and odd circumstances sometimes combine to upset man's calculations, however. Roof collapses in heavy snow years are not a rarity in cottage country.

There are few things more heartbreaking than seeing a roof caved in by snow. Smart cottagers who have shingled roofs and want wintertime peace of mind make the upward trek with shovel in hand and clear the roof snow, just in case. Those who can't make the climb reach for their wallets and hire roof shovellers.

Another option is the snow rake, plastic or metal blades attached to extendable handles. You can drag soft snow off your roof with these without too much effort. They come in a variety of shapes and sizes for different applications. Snow raking the roof makes a good excuse for summer cottagers to make a winter visit.

It's stuff like this that we learn every day at the cottage. The lessons are mostly about nature and how to live safely and comfortably within its rules. Cottagers know that the best way to understand the forces of nature is to witness them.

The most common lessons involve water. Water is the raison d'être for most cottages. Swimming, boating, fishing. Summer fun and all that. It's ironic then that water is among the cottager's worst enemies, especially in rocky hill country like Ontario's Laurentian Shield where Shaman's Rock is located. Water has a one-track mind telling it: get to an ocean. It will go around, over, under, or through anything that is in its way. It will carry off obstacles to its progress.

You can't eliminate water at the cottage. You learn how it travels, its tricks, and how to redirect it to avoid its impacts. If you don't, you suffer cottage horrors such as roof leaks, cottage rot, unstable foundations, and sundry forms of washouts.

Water and March winds are nature's mop and bucket for cleaning up winter's dregs. It's not long before the land sparkles with spring freshness. Nature has set a good example and I follow it, diving head-first into an ocean of spring chores. Soon I'm raking, sweeping, and washing, then gluing, patching, and reinforcing the vent stack. Extra screws secure the steel snow guard, which must remain bent until someone stronger comes along. Then it's on to the routine. Winter shovels go inside, summer shovels and rakes come out. There is outdoor furniture to inspect, recondition, and paint.

The postage stamp lawn needs a raking, but this year there is no damage from moles digging for grubs. Diane, my wife and cottage soulmate, sprinkled the grass with castor oil last fall and it seems to have worked. Some of the experts say it doesn't, but we don't have any mole damage.

A lawn is an anomaly at the cottage. We don't need things that make a cottage look like a place in the city. However, we have compromised with a tiny, fifty square metre lawn at Shaman's Rock, just to hold down the buckets of dirt that get tracked into the cottage. It provides a patch on which kids and dogs can romp freely without crashing into rocks or dragging themselves through dirt. Besides, you usually need something to cover the cottage septic field.

The thought of kids and dogs is another reminder that there is much work to do before summer. Bugs, kids, cottage dogs, and summer visitors demand attention that takes away from cottage work, which for many cottagephiles is one of the great joys of cottaging.

Spring is too short a season.

— 2 —
ICE OUT!

"I remember a hundred lovely lakes, and recall the fragrant
breath of pine and fir...."
— HAMLIN GARLAND, AMERICAN NOVELIST

The sounds of spring erupt on every forest ridge and in every gully. A warming wind sighs in tree branches still stiff from winter's paralysis. Water gurgles through every low spot, so happy to have been transformed from the prison of ice into liquid freedom.

Runoff from Fagan's Ponds, which sit high above the cliffs across the lake, races down through crevices and small canyons, creating a dull roar heard around the lake. Mixing with the roar are the occasional groans and cracks of the lake ice expanding and contracting. Sound carries beyond the hills now that mufflers of snow have disappeared and the hardwoods on the back hills are still bare of leaves. Just beyond the ponds is a swampy area to which the herons will soon return to rebuild their nests in the treetops and lay the eggs of their new generation.

The loudest sounds are the calls of the crows and ravens, cawing and croaking messages among themselves and warnings to other forest creatures smart enough to listen and understand them. Surely these are the cleverest of the animals. They wait, watch, and think, never doing anything that will place them at a disadvantage. I call out to one of several crows raising a racket from the safety of the treetops.

"Bekkayaun, Aandek!" I shout in the Algonquian tongue of the people who occupied this forest centuries before cottagers. "Be quiet, crow."

He stares down at me, amusement shining from black eyes that are small and beady and intelligently boastful. He knows the truth: for all that I do with my buildings, my tools, and my toys, I am insignificant. I am but a passing shadow.

Then I see the cause of the beaking off. A pathetic little red fox is standing on a grey granite slab just off to the side of the bird feeders. He has come in hopes of catching a bird or squirrel feeding off seed that has spilled to the ground. *Good luck with that*, I muse. He is weak and slow. Mange has rotted most of his once bushy tail, giving him the look of a shaved poodle with a pom-pom tail. He is painfully thin and when he moves, I notice he limps.

He sees me but is too sick to care about a possible human threat. I back away, leaving him to his hunting, but knowing he will not catch much or survive long. Life is wonderful out here, but it can be sadly cruel.

It's a joy to be outside now that winter has receded. The senses are sharper. The sights, sounds, and smells of a new season are everywhere. You can smell the earth's dampness drying in the spring sun. It is a warm, humid smell combining the odours of winter's rot with the newness of micro-organisms stirring to life in the soil. It is a smell distinct from any other, not easy to describe, but somewhat close to the smell of wet wool mittens drying near the woodstove.

You also can smell the rotting ice. A pungent, wet smell, neither obnoxious nor pleasant. It is a fusty odour in your nostrils announcing major change is underway. The ice is nearing its final stage of life. It rots daily in the strengthening sun and when its winter white turns to a black-blue it is just about finished.

On our lake — St. Nora Lake — the ice usually leaves during the second or third week of April, except in 2010 when it slipped away April Fool's Day, an unheard-of early date that was blamed immediately on global warming. Maybe global warming is part of it, maybe not. Every year is different. In 2011 it lingered until the final days of April.

Predicting "ice out" is a competitive cottage sport. Cottagers who have jobs during the week always hope it will happen on a weekend because there is something magical about seeing the last of it go. In some cottage areas there are betting pools on when the ice will leave.

Ice out is wrapped in myths. Some believe the ice sinks and disappears at one particular moment. Actually it just melts gradually and is broken up by the wind into large floating sheets that gradually disappear. Each year breakup is different depending on temperatures and wind. Sometimes large patches shift up and down the lake, seemingly hanging around forever. Other years you'll see a vast expanse of blue-black just before dark, then awake the next morning to millions of sunbeams dancing on the lake's ripples.

"Aw, we missed it," Diane cries as we drive past the Leslie Frost Centre where St. Nora Lake meets Highway 35 just south of Dorset. The north bay of the lake is sparkling blue. When we left here ten days ago, there was solid white-blue ice. We are both disappointed because we had hoped to sit on our lakeside deck and watch the ice go out.

A different scene greets us when we pull into the cottage driveway. The lake section we see from our cottage is covered by a thin, rotting ice sheet pushed into the south half of the lake by a north breeze. We didn't miss it after all.

Sketch by Zita Poling Moynan.

When the ice breaks up at Shaman's Rock in April, cottage country is once again set free and renewed life is seen from an outside deck.

Soon after we arrive, the breeze turns and becomes a stiff wind from the south. We sit at the shore and watch the ice being pushed north, pieces of it breaking up and disappearing before our eyes. Within two hours the lake is completely clear. The winter that was here such a short time ago is gone. Once again we are fortunate enough to witness the most dramatic scene in the miracle of spring at the cottage.

We want to savour it, so after supper we light a campfire and sit overlooking the newly uncovered lake. The moon peeks above the rocky hills across the lake and soon its beams are bouncing brightly on the darkened waters. The moonbeams are matched by a million blinking stars. I sit wearing just a t-shirt. At nine p.m. it is nineteen degrees Celsius. Rare are such perfect nights even at the height of summer.

We savour the stillness and tranquility because tomorrow we must turn our minds to the many tasks of spring.

— 3 —
ST. NORA

"The sun was warm but the wind was chill.
You know how it is with an April day."
— ROBERT FROST

Gearing oneself for spring chores takes strength of mind as well as body. Distractions are everywhere. Only a steely focus can drive off the temptations to fish, explore the spring woods, watch a downy woodpecker extract bugs from a patient and giving hemlock, or simply sit on a rock and consume the scenery.

Today my focus is not steely. It is too spring-like to jump into chores. The sun is bright and happy, and everything around me seems new and happening for the first time. It isn't, of course, because this change from winter to spring has been witnessed many thousands of times by the people who have gone before.

Springs long past have seen Indians collecting maple sap in birch bark vessels, and fishing for lake trout coming up from the winter depths. These woods also were alive long ago with the crashing and thumping of trees falling, shrieking of sawmill whistles, and the neighing of horses brought in to help with the heavy labour of harvesting the thick forests. My relatively recent springs here have been quiet in comparison.

St. Nora Lake sits on the edges of different worlds. A rock toss west and northwest of it is the famed Muskoka Lakes country, Ontario's outdoor recreation jewel. It reflects the wealth, power, and bustle of Toronto, the country's largest urban core. Many Muskoka cottages are mansions that fetch resale prices into the millions of dollars.

East is Haliburton, a bit off the trodden path, less expensive and with a more blue-collar cottage past. North and northeast is Algonquin Park, a monument to the people who decided more than a century ago that it should be reserved as a park for all the people.

Dorset hamlet on Lake of Bays, and at the intersection of Highways 117 and 35, stands with one foot in Muskoka District and the other in Haliburton County. South of Dorset, and running past St. Nora Lake, Highway 35 divides Muskoka and Haliburton.

The setting is a wilderness of natural riches, hundreds of lakes, streams, rocky vistas, and stands of pine, birch, poplar, and hard-woods. It was the majestic white pines, painted often by Canadian artists that caught the attention of the European pioneers. The thick and tall white pines made excellent ship masts during the tall-ship sailing heydays of the 1800s. Thousands fell to loggers' axes before being shipped out along newly built wilderness rail lines to ships that carried them down the St. Lawrence River and off to shipyards in Britain and the United States.

St. Nora Lake might have slumbered on the edge of this lumber-ing boom except for an unlikely business scheme put together by the Gilmour Lumber Co. of Trenton. In 1892, the year before Algonquin Park was established, the Gilmour brothers bought the logging rights to almost 23,000 hectares of forest around Canoe and Tea Lakes in what would become the park. At three-quarters-of-a-million dollars it was a rich buy, but with much promise of profit. Lumberman David Gilmour had one problem: how best to get the logs from Canoe Lake to his mill in Trenton on Lake Ontario, more than 400 kilometres south.

He could have floated the logs down into Lake of Bays, then along the water system into Georgian Bay, then down into Lake Ontario and along to Trenton. That's a long, tortuous journey. Gilmour chose another route, based on an odd geographic fact of the Dorset area.

Roughly three to four kilometres south of Dorset is a height of land that marks the division of two watersheds. One is the Lake of Bays–Muskoka River system into Georgian Bay. The other is the Trent system, of which St. Nora Lake and nearby Raven Lake are two main lakes at its source.

Gilmour decided to float a million logs down the Oxtongue River from Tea Lake into Lake of Bays and boom and tow them to Dorset. Once there, they were ten kilometres north of the watershed that flows down to Trenton. But how to get them beyond that height of land blocking access to the Trent system?

Gilmour opted for a fantastic plan of building a mechanical tramway to transport the logs over the hills beyond Dorset and into Raven and St. Nora lakes and the Trent-Severn water system. His crews constructed a wooden tramway that ran up a forty-metre incline from just outside Dorset. Once up the hill, they built a dam, diverted and reversed water flow, and jackladdered and floated logs down to Raven Lake.

Various dams and ditches were built to allow the logs to be floated out of Raven, down the Black River into Wren Lake and through a ditch and swamp that ran down what is now Highway 35 to St. Nora Lake where the Frost Centre now stands. Once in St. Nora, the logs could follow waterways down into Lake Ontario to be boomed and towed to Gilmour's Trenton mills.

The tramway worked reasonably well. However, it took two years for the logs to travel from Tea Lake to Trenton, where they arrived much beaten up by rapids and rocks. The route was not fast enough or efficient enough to support a profitable operation. The timing was against Gilmour. Steam was ending the tall ships era and the market for logs had dwindled. The scheme was a financial disaster.

So for a brief time Dorset area had an important spot in the Canadian economy. It was a time of booming activity: steam-operated alligators pulling and pushing log booms through the lakes, the rattle and splashing of the tramway, the shouts of men clearing snagged logs in the trenches and streams. Some people say that hundreds of logs, strays from the drives, still rest on the bottom of St. Nora Lake.

I knew nothing of all this when I stumbled through the area in the mid-1980s by accident. I had never heard of Dorset, or any Christian saint named St. Nora, probably because there is none. No one seems to know the original name or how it morphed into the name of a non-existent saint.

The name on early maps was Senora or Sonora. Some people believe *sonora* was an Ojibwe word because the Ojibwe Indians occupied the area. Sonora does not resemble any Ojibwe word that I know, although it is possible that it is an unrecognizable mangling of some Indian word. After all, Longfellow managed to get Gitchee Gummee out of the Ojibwe/Chippewa name for Great Lake: Gitchee Gammee. More likely, the name had Spanish origins. Sonora in Spanish indicates sound and some people suggested it related to the echoes off the cliffs on the lake's east side. Sonora probably grew out of *señora*, the Spanish word often applied to the Virgin Mary. Someone dropped the accent and the E changed to O and we got sonora. It has happened before. Sonora, Mexico, and presumably the Sonoran Desert are names created from Mexican references to the señora, the Virgin.

There is Spanish influence in the area. Orillia, just south of St. Nora, is said to come from the Spanish word *orilla*, meaning shore or a lake or river. Then there's Mariposa, Spanish for butterfly, and Oro, Spanish for gold.

The Geographical Names Board of Canada didn't really care where the name came from and officially recognized the lake as St. Nora in 1947. Not St. Nora's or Lake St. Nora. Just St. Nora Lake.

St. Nora is a smallish lake, roughly two or three kilometres wide and three kilometres long. A tight, shallow narrows connects its south end to Kushog Lake, which runs another fifteen kilometres north to south. Its main feature is soaring cliffs on the inaccessible east shore, magnificent rock faces adorned by white pines, hemlocks, and oaks. The water off the cliffs is twenty metres deep, forty-plus metres deep in the middle of the lake.

You can get a peek at the cliffs from Highway 35, the 200-kilometre north-south link that connects Highway 60 just east of Huntsville with the Kawartha Lakes area just north of Highway 401. Highway 35 touches St. Nora briefly at the Leslie Frost Centre. The highway has been there for almost eighty years, having been started in the south in 1930 as a Depression-era project to create jobs. Road workers stayed in huts built along the route. The cabins at Ox Narrows Lodge on Kushog Lake, just south of St. Nora, are said to be the original workers' huts. The narrows got its name when a team of oxen fell through the ice and drowned.

In 1909, Hamilton Killally Woodruff of St. Catharines bought the seventy-five-acre island in St. Nora for fifty cents an acre and named it

Margaret Island, after his daughter. Somehow it became St. Margaret Island, the name registered by the Geographical Names Board. Woodruff later bought the tiny island in the middle of the lake and it became known as Woodruff Island. The Woodruffs also owned a large patch of land where the highway touches the lake.

St. Margaret Island developed into quite a summer colony. There was a large main house with five bedrooms and at least three fireplaces. There was a tennis court, three boat houses, stone pump house, and stone cool house. A second log cabin was built for servants. There were cows, horses, chickens, and other livestock.

The Woodruffs were a wealthy, historic, and famous family on the Niagara Peninsula. H.K.'s dad was Samuel Woodruff, superintendent of the Welland Canal and one of St. Catharines' wealthiest men. H.K.'s daughter Margaret, who married Percy Band, began selling off the St. Nora Lake holdings in the 1940s.

In 1944 she sold forty-three acres on the lake at Highway 35 to the University of Toronto. This land later became the site of the Ontario Forest Ranger School and later the Leslie Frost Centre. In 1947 she sold St. Margaret and Woodruff islands to a group who built Camp Comak, a summer camp for boys. That camp was closed in the early 1970s and the island subdivided for approximately forty private cottage lots.

One of the workers who helped Margaret Woodruff Band wrap up the Woodruff colony on the island was Harold Sedgwick, a bush worker, lumber mill hand, and handyman. He built a cabin on St. Nora across from the island in 1932, then married and built a two-storey house in 1939. It's still there, including the asbestos siding shingles that Mrs. Band gave him off one of the island buildings he tore down for her.

Harold was a last link with St. Nora's early history. He was in his early eighties when I first knew him. He used to walk the cottage road snowmobile track in winter, a tall, gaunt man with sunken eyes peering out from a frosted fur-trim parka hood. He was failing then, having a tough time keeping the big place heated, and sometimes a tougher time trying to articulate the many wonders he had seen in his decades in the bush around the lake. I was sad that a man so attuned to bush life and the history of the area had to fade away.

Mainland cottaging on St. Nora began mainly as the result of Camp Comak. A few cottages dotted the shoreline near the Comak Landing at Highway 35. The road at first ended at Harold Sedgewick's place. Most of the land beyond that was owned by an Irish-Canadian farmer called Jack Kinnear who owned a large piece of the lakefront that extended out to Highway 35 to his farmhouse. Kinnear sold pieces of the lakefront to various people, notably Charlie and Rita Aquilina in 1970 and the Gilbert family soon after. The road did not extend all the way down the shoreline then and the Aquilinas and Gilberts had to make their own rough tracks.

The Aquilinas, Gilberts, plus the Malloys, Winches, Grants, and Lehmans were among the early cottagers. In the mid-1980s you could still see Harold puttering about his two-storey house. Or tall old Mr. Winch, then in his nineties, still cutting up branches with a buck saw. So was Mr. Lehman, cutting and piling as he kept an eye on his wife, who had Alzheimer's and had to wear a life jacket outside the cottage because she sometimes lost track of time and place and wandered. All of these folks were fixtures on the road when I stumbled across St. Nora Lake by accident.

Back in the 1980s I used to take off once in the spring and once in the fall to get out of the city and tour cottage country properties. I missed our first cottage on Mink Lake, near Eganville in the Ottawa Valley, which we sold when my job took us to Vancouver. We loved that cottage, but the distance between Vancouver and Eganville made keeping it impractical.

When we returned east, my biannual excursions into cottage country north of Toronto were therapeutic, not potential buying trips. I had no intention of buying another cottage, but did have a burning hurt somewhere deep inside over giving up the first one.

What happened on one spring excursion was Diane's fault. A friend had told her about a lovely little cottage on the Muskoka River south of Huntsville. It apparently carried a ridiculously low price tag: an absolute steal. They both were curious about what the place would sell for, and I was assigned the task of checking it out during my ramblings.

I arrived at a dark, dank spot in a cedar grove along the Muskoka River.

It was difficult to see the cottage for sale, but you could see a large place immediately across the river. The river was no more than thirty-fives metres wide, so close you could see into the other place's windows.

It was difficult to breathe without consuming dozens of mosquitoes and blackflies. I fled, without really seeing the offered cottage, which was consumed by jungle-like vegetation.

I stopped into a realty office in Huntsville because I had promised to bring back an idea of what the owners actually would take for the Muskoka River place. A pleasant young man gave me all the details and started a sales pitch that I immediately shot down with a rant about my dislike for low dark places in the cedars. I was a Northern Ontario boy. Rock faces, airy forests, great vistas.

"You want a high place? Rocks? I've got one for you. Down Highway 35 just south of Dorset. "

I explained I didn't really want anything. I was just out enjoying the scenery.

"You can drive back to the city that way. Just a couple hundred yards south of the Frost Centre you'll see the lake. Just turn left onto a muddy road. You have a four-wheel drive, so you'll be okay."

I'd never been on Highway 35 so I took it on the way home. I found the cottage road and it was as miserable as he had warned. One kilometre in through the mud I found the "For Sale" sign. There was a parking spot cut into the lot, heavily forested enough to conceal its steep hills. There was a small rock face just back from the shoreline, and you had to climb down to get to the lake.

As soon as I got my truck out of the muddy road I called the salesman and bought the lot over the telephone. I still don't know why. Maybe I blacked out for a few minutes, or was struck temporarily insane by the black flies.

"You did what?" was Diane's reaction when I returned home. "Are you crazy? What are we going to do with a lot in the bush?"

The entire family was convinced I had lost my mind. They insisted that we go on the next available weekend to see this folly.

The cottage road was not so passable for Diane's two-wheel-drive station wagon. I met cottager Charlie Aquilina, who had been on the lake since the 1970s, and had extended the road into his lot. He offered me his boat and motor so I could give the family a tour of the shoreline.

Luckily I was carrying a small bush axe when we arrived at our shore. I hacked my way through the bush, clearing a path for the family to crawl up the hill to a flat spot where someone had built a campfire pit and an outhouse. Diane was in tears.

"You will never, ever build anything on this, this ... rocky hill."

The children were silent, shuffling their feet, worry flickering in their eyes. In me they saw Jack Torrance, the madman caretaker of the Overlook Hotel in the movie *The Shining*, who beats his way through a door with an axe and tells his wife, "Wendy, I'm home!"

They were not far wrong. Bush axe in hand I clambered up the granite mound at the lot's north edge and peered out over the lake. I had to calm them so I told them that an Ojibwe shaman once used this rocky spot for meditation and visions. This would be our place for visions!

Photograph by the author.

The site of Shaman's Rock was a wall of trees beside the lake when we first saw it more than twenty-five years ago. Now it's the dream come true, a place of our own in the Canadian bush country.

"Diane, we're home!"

So, we had arrived at Shaman's Rock, St. Nora Lake, the beginning of a new era in our lives — one not without incidents. We cleared the lot that summer with two chainsaws, one rented and one bought new. I left my new chainsaw on the ground while I dropped a large oak with the larger, rented one. The oak made a direct hit on the bought chainsaw, smashing it into a dozen pieces. We ate our meals in a dining tent filled with mosquitoes. Diane and I slept Friday and Saturday nights in the back of the pickup truck. She caught pneumonia. I broke my shoulder.

This is the best of Laurentian Shield Country, and there is a lot of rock that gets in the way. We built bonfires on it, then scraped away the coals and poured ice-cold water on it to make it break. That's what Hannibal did to get his armies across the Alps, but he used water mixed with sour wine. We drank ours.

The cottage went up next fall. It was small and boxlike, but we kicked up a side wall that allowed us to build a loft for extra space. Month by month, year by year the place took shape and became a real cottage.

Like most cottagers, we were keeners. The cottage road was not open in winter, not passable until early May. So we brought in the toilet, bathtub, sink, and vanity by wheelbarrow over the snowmobile track. I dragged dock barrels over the ice and built a dock with battery-operated tools. It sat on the ice waiting for spring thaw.

Wonderful memories. However, reflecting on the past doesn't get the chores done. And there are always plenty to get done to put our place on summer footing.

— 4 —
WOOD CHIPS

"People love chopping wood. In this activity one immediately
sees results."
— ALBERT EINSTEIN

Something is stalking me while I do spring cottage chores. It is always there, staring out from the forest's edge, prodding my subconscious. Even when I am in bed at night it's there, big and brooding like an unhappy bear standing in the corner. I wish I could do what Inuit hunters do when confronted at close range by an unhappy bear: punch it in the nose. Bears, by all accounts, are confused by a hard whack on the snout. That's no help in my case because the thing stalking me is a mirage. Only one action will make it go away — finish all the smaller chores, throw back my shoulders, and start swinging an axe.

The bruin in the room is the ghost of the woodpile on the other side of the driveway. Last year it was a magnificent stack of split hardwood, almost five metres long, 1.2 metres high, and three .40-metre rows deep. That's one that's easier in Imperial: sixteen feet long, four feet high, and three sixteen-inch rows. Six fireplace cords, two full bush cords. When the sun shone on its fresh cut ends, the pile looked like stacked bricks of gold. A well-kept woodpile is as good as gold.

Now it's a sad, gap-toothed space with a few crooked rows leaning tiredly against one another. If there is to be heat in the cottage during next winter's visits, the empty space must become new fresh ends of cut and split hardwood set to dry and cure.

Most people get next winter's firewood before the current winter ends. The snow makes it easier to haul the logs out of the bush. Splitting and stacking in March allows a minimum time for the wood to lose its wet greenness, and to be ready to burn when winter returns. Ideally, wood should dry for a year. The perfect scenario is to split and stack in March wood that will not be needed until eighteen months ahead. By then you have rock-solid cured wood that burns hot, but slowly, when the stove or fireplace is choked down.

Ideally the moisture content of firewood should be 15 to 20 percent. By comparison, kiln-dried lumber for construction has a moisture content of 10 percent. Drier wood burns more quickly, of course, and wood with more than 20 percent moisture tends to smoulder.

Wood hunting as the snow leaves the forest is one of my favourite cottage activities. Without snow or leaves, the forest is open and you get a clear view of the hummocks, pockets, and ridges obscured much of the year. It's easy to spot the deadfalls, windfalls, and standing dead trees that provide a feast for the wood hunter.

The spring woods hold a cornucopia of potential firewood, but the wood hunter must be careful that one's eyes are not bigger than one's muscles. A beautiful beech blown down on that far ridge looks like a treasure, but you still have to cut it up, lug out the pieces, and transport them before you even begin the cutting into rounds, splitting, and stacking.

Wood is amazing stuff. Take oak. Oak blowdowns or oak standing dead are treasures. They take years to rot. More than a decade ago my bush lot was logged and some logs were left behind. I found them a year or so ago and they were still hard on the inside and made a good addition to the woodpile.

It's easy to be over-enthusiastic about firewood. Some years back I had open-heart surgery to fix a birth defect too risky to repair until new technology and technique came along. The surgeon anticipated a difficult operation, and it was. We all got through it pretty much okay. I went back to the surgeon for a six-week assessment and asked about resuming some normal activities, including going to the cottage.

"What do you plan to do there?" he asked.

"Well, it's April and I need to start cutting my firewood," I replied.

"Cutting firewood?"

"Yes, I need to put it up soon so it will be dry for next winter."

He paused, looked at my wife, then back to me.

"Let me see if I fully understand this. Six weeks ago you spent eight hours on the operating table. We had a hard fight to pull you through. When you did pull through we discovered you had lost sight in your right eye. Now six weeks later you want to go into the woods with a sharp axe and start cutting firewood. Does that sound reasonable to you?"

I guess he had a point, but I don't think he fully appreciated the importance of having a well-stacked woodpile curing in the summer sun. A woodpile is security; maturing and ready for use when the cold, dark days come.

Doing firewood is important, but it never seems right to go wood hunting without having the waterfront set up for summer. Cottages are all about the waterfront, and getting the shore ready first, after all urgent repairs are done, is a priority. The tin boat has to be turned over and wrestled into the water. The motor, gas can, oars, and other accessories are pulled from storage, then it's out onto the water to tow back the floating docks, which are kept in a protected bay where they are less likely to be crushed by travelling lake ice.

I dream of a new, easier-to-handle dock system, something with aluminum framing and lighter than the wooden docks and ramp I have now. But there is little time for dreaming at this time of year. A decision needs to be made on bringing in firewood.

With the docks set in place, and a bit of summer furniture set out, I feel less guilty about striking out on a wood hunt.

There are three choices: find, cut up, and haul in forest deadfalls; order a load of logs from a local logger; or order firewood cut split and delivered from a woodcutter. It's a choice between spending money and suffering bodily pain. We opt for bodily pain to save money.

There is always some logging underway on Crown land around us and I am dismayed how they take the trunks and leave huge hardwood crowns to rot in the bush. This mess is a fire hazard, blocks access for anyone travelling the bush, and is a shameful waste. Years ago I began cutting up the fallen tops for firewood and grabbing any windfalls that happened to be around.

Ranger Bob, my name for any provincial government official in cottage country, does not see my point of view, and insists on selling permits for the gathering of deadfalls. I ran into him one day at the Leslie Frost Centre, when it was still a government operation. I mentioned that I had just finished getting my spring wood. Beautiful stuff. Hardwood crowns left to rot in the bush. Big mistake.

"I don't remember you getting a permit," he said.

"Permit? I need a permit for cleaning up the woods?"

He lectured me on the latest forest management techniques, and reminded me to buy a government permit every time I took a piece of fallen tree from Crown land. I nodded understanding, then silently vowed to become the Robin Hood of the woodstove set, stealing every stick of wood I could from the king to warm the hearths of me and my friends.

As it turned out, I didn't have to become a criminal to get my winter wood. A wonderful woodlot went up for sale behind the cottage and we bought it. There I get all the firewood I need for free and manage my little forest at the same time.

Doing firewood stresses the muscles but cools the mind. What is more satisfying than sitting on a stump, taking off work gloves, and gazing contentedly at a freshly stacked woodpile? What you see are genuine assets created by your own toil: dozens of squared off, neatly placed pieces that will keep you warm in winter.

A well-managed woodpile is like having money in the bank. Loggers know that. They have seen the firewood market flourish as other rising energy costs make firewood production more cost effective. More people are using wood heat as the price of heating oil, propane and electricity goes higher. Canada Mortgage and Housing Corp. estimates that more than one million Canadian families use wood as a primary or supplementary heating fuel.

On country roads outside the urban areas you can't help noticing the growing stacks of firewood in people's yards. Throughout cottage country you see more and more gnarly looking guys in checkered jack shirts running chainsaws and swinging mauls in side yards and on woodlots.

"Firewood represents the simplest opportunity for connecting the forest resource to the energy market at the retail level," Leo Hall, manager of Opeongo Forestry Service in Renfrew, told *The Working Forest* newspaper some time back. "You don't need to make a big investment in fancy factories to process the fuel. Essentially you can take it straight from the bush to the market to compete with fossil fuels and others."

Similarly, Wade Knight, executive director for the Ontario Woodlot Association, was quoted as saying more woodlot owners are turning to firewood sales. "A lot of our members are having no problem selling their wood," said Knight. "A few of our members have seen a 25-per-cent increase in what they could sell it for."

Wood ready to burn goes for around $100 a fireplace cord in our area. You can buy a load of logs for $800 and cut and split them yourself. A load produces about seventeen fireplace cords. So that's just under $50 a cord, plus your labour.

Around Shaman's Rock we are lucky to have an abundance of hardwood. Ash, oak, hard maple, beech, and birch provide the best burning characteristics and the most British thermal units (BTUs), which is a measurement of the heat produced when fuels are burned. Hardwoods often are the easiest to split. Red oak and beech is straight grained with few knots and splits nicely, even when green. Ironwood, or hornbeam, a high heat output wood, is difficult to split and does not burn as easily as the others.

Cottages in areas where hardwood is not plentiful burn softwoods like poplar, tamarack, and pine. These are not the best burners but you have to take what is available.

Whenever I've let my wood supply get dangerously low I borrow a hydraulic wood splitter. But when time and weather are with me, swinging maul for a couple of hours tightens the muscles and loosens the tensions of the mind. I like a maul for splitting because it is heavier than a standard axe and its wedge-like head forces the wood apart. An axe tends to sink into the wood without much splitting pressure, especially if it is not swung properly.

I'm not Hulk Hogan, but no one has to be to split firewood. In wood splitting, much like golf, technique trumps brute strength. Mauls usually come in six- or eight-pound weights and even heavier. I find the six-pound easier to swing, easier to accelerate on the downswing. Like golf, the downswing is where you want the power.

The edge of a maul does not need to be sharpened like an axe, which is a good thing for me because I've never been able to sharpen anything properly, including pencils. The maul's purpose is to split the wood by forcing it apart.

I stare a lot at the round I am about to split. And it's not because I'm just buying time to catch my breath between swings. Concentrated aim makes wood splitting easier (as well as helping you keep all your toes). Just like golf, the idea is to keep your eye on the ball. I want to land the blow exactly where I want it.

Starting at the edge of larger rounds makes the work much simpler. Once I break off one edge piece from the round, the rest of the breaking comes easier. I avoid aiming at the far outer edge of the round because striking just beyond the edge can lead to a broken handle, or even a broken wrist. Also, a very slight wrist snap on the downswing brings the maul down on an angle, which helps break the wood apart.

The hardest part of wood splitting is trying to excite interest in others — children, grandchildren, visitors. Most people do not share my enthusiasm for the woodpile. When I do corral someone I try to start them with splitting smaller rounds. We like sixteen-inch lengths in firewood, but I go down to twelve inches to make splitting easier for the newbies. I also encourage them to split on another round or some hard surface. A soft surface, like the ground, absorbs energy from the maul blow, energy that should be directed into the wood.

These are valuable lessons, given absolutely for free, but few people, if any, ever come back for more.

Wood heat is not for all cottagers. After we sold our first cottage on Mink Lake near Eganville, the first thing the new owners did was remove the two woodstoves, one a typical heating woodstove, the other a beautiful old cook stove. They didn't want the hassles of woodstoves: hauling and storing wood, safety issues, and insurance demands.

Heating with wood is hard, messy work. Tools must be looked after, chainsaw kept in sharp running order, and the mechanical wood splitter, if you have one, must be maintained.

Firewood must be stacked properly, out of the wet, yet exposed enough to let the wind dry and cure it. It's not a good idea to stack it on your deck, against a cottage wall or anywhere close to the cottage. Yes, against the wall outside the door is handy on those cold, snowy mornings. But firewood is home sweet home for insects and other vermin like mice, snakes, and carpenter ants. You don't want those critters near the cottage walls. It's okay to have a small log rack within handy distance of your woodstove. The bulk of your firewood, however, is best kept in an open-ended wood shed on which it can be stacked off the ground, and well away from the cottage.

The most active and hardest to detect chewers at the cottage are the carpenter ants. They are bigger ants, six to twenty-five millimetres long, and identified by their narrow waists and antennae that are bent in the middle. They mate during the heat of summer and the queen and males each have two wings during that time.

They can do major damage to a cottage, chewing door and window frames and structural framework that can cost thousands of dollars to replace. At least one cottager friend we know found out about a carpenter ant invasion when it was too late and the repair bill, mostly for hidden damage, was in the tens of thousands of dollars.

Carpenter ants love moist and decaying wood. So if you have them, it's not good enough just to eliminate them. You must eliminate the moisture and its source or the ants will keep coming back.

They leave little piles of coarse sawdust where they are active, but often you don't see it because they are active in out-of-sight places, like behind walls. The best prevention is check with your local hardware store on sprays and how to use them, or call a pest control company.

Firewood also brings the frustrations of government regulations and insurance. It's really important for cottagers with woodstoves to ensure that their insurance company is fully aware and happy with any wood burning appliances. New installations must be done by someone with WETT (Wood Energy Technology Transfer) certification.

Once you satisfy government and insurance company rules for wood burning, you still are responsible for proper maintenance. Chimneys must be kept clean to avoid chimney fires. The best way to avoid those is to burn hot fires. Bigger is not necessarily better in woodstoves. You want one that is slightly undersized for your cottage. Too big means you'll be dampening the fire to hold down the heat, creating more smoke and creosote build-up in the chimney.

We clean our chimney once a year. We pull a chimney brush through, but some people just run a heavy chain down the chimney and rattle it about to knock the soot build-up free. We have to climb up on the roof to do that, and when we do we inspect the wire mesh around the chimney cap. It rots, leaving holes for squirrels to get in.

Flying squirrels got into our place one year by crawling through rotted mesh. They went down the chimney and into the woodstove. They found their way through the baffles and out into the cottage. There is no need to detail the mess they created, except to say they chewed a trophy fish that I had mounted for display on a wall.

Woodstove door seals have to be checked as well. You can test the effectiveness of the seal by closing the door on a currency bill. If the bill pulls free easily once the door is shut, you should consider replacing the gasket. Rope gaskets and glue can be bought many places and are easy to use.

The same applies to firebricks that line most woodstoves. They deteriorate over time. Replacements are fairly standard, easy to find, and uncomplicated to install.

One annoying thing about woodstoves is that door glass will brown up and block your view of a pleasant fire. We burn hot fires to try to avoid this, but it still happens sometimes. We clean the glass with wet newspaper dipped in ash. I find the glass cleans easiest when it is hot. Some people use razor blades to scratch woodstove glass clean. It works but is awkward and can scratch the glass.

New technologies have made wood burning much more efficient, less environmentally damaging, and more pleasurable. Newer stoves are designed to burn more efficiently, with less particulate discharge up the stack and more heat from warm air convection than just heat radiation. They are a far cry from the old barrel stoves that singed a lot of kids' mittens at outdoor skating rinks around the country.

There are demands now for government to prohibit wood burning. Organized groups are campaigning to ban all wood stoves, no matter how much the technology has improved. Stop all wood burning. Period.

This has touched off a small war pitting burners again anti-burners. It would have been too much to ask, I guess, that if there had to be a war of words, that it be civil, thoughtful, and a bit intelligent. Such is not the case as evidenced by this editorial in the *Woodsmoke Activist Newsletter*: "For as many years as I have been researching the psyches of burners, I have not come up with why they have the need to hurt others. I know it is there but I can't put my finger on it yet. Some have suggested pyromania, control issues, mental illnesses and even a wood fetish."

So, I'm mentally ill because I burn wood to heat my cottage? Well, perhaps I just want to keep warm, like other humans who discovered fire many thousands of years ago and have been burning wood ever since.

This is the kind of stuff that drives country people crazy. Growing trees absorb carbon dioxide from the air and store it as carbon. Dead wood releases carbon dioxide back into the atmosphere whether it burns or not. When a tree falls over and dies, its rotting process releases carbon dioxide and other gases. Everything around us has some bad effect. Wood at least is renewable and its use is being well managed to reduce its negative effects on our world.

As Frank Lloyd Wright, the acclaimed American "organic architect," once said: "The best friend on earth of man is the tree: When we use the tree respectfully and economically, we have one of the greatest resources of the earth."

The same people demanding that all wood burning be banned are just like the rest of us — huge consumers of fossil fuels, electricity, plastics, paints, cleaning chemicals, metals, electronic parts, and all the other gazillion things that impact our planet. A daily bowel movement has an impact on the planet. Get over it and get on with some thoughtful, important actions that can stop the many horrors we see daily in our world.

Let's all take deep breath, relax in front of the woodstove and listen to Jimi Hendrix singing: "I have only one burning desire / Let me stand next to your fire."

— 5 —
MATING

"The loons! The loons! They're welcoming us back."
— KATHARINE HEPBURN IN *ON GOLDEN POND*

Everything around the lake comes alive as it throws off winter's shackles. Boats appear at the Highway 35 landing and sounds of sawing, hammering, and wood splitting float across the lake from St. Margaret Island, a cottaging colony that depends on open water or solid ice for access.

The woods along the lake's shores awaken from winter sleep. The black bear up the hill is out of her winter den, pawing moodily through the hardwoods in search of acorns, insect larvae, or anything else that will soothe the gnawing hunger in her stomach until new greenery appears. We hope she stays up the hill and does not venture down to our bird feeders. Last spring she seemed desperate for food and made destructive nightly visits until I had to put two shotguns blasts over her head. That was only after she had left paw and nose prints on one of the main windows.

The chipmunks are not moody and unpredictable like the bears. They are more numerous, but comical and less destructive, generally content to stay out of the bird feeders and eat the seed that spills to the ground. When they are not eating, they chase each other through the dead oak leaves that crunch like potato chips. Occasionally one will stop to stare at me, wondering what business I have there.

They do dig holes, sometimes in places where we do not want them. I tried getting them to relocate a rather large and busy hole, but they refused. So I tried some popular persuaders: moth balls, hot red pepper, human hair cuttings. None of these worked, but castor oil did.

The red squirrels are more businesslike. They are busy searching for food, casing the bird feeders, and planning new ways of getting into the cottage eaves. They are never too busy, however, to stop to give you an earful of cheeky trills.

Mating sounds are in the air. In the ravine carrying a small freshet to the lake I hear the quick, urgent gobble of a Tom wooing a hen turkey. It is not a loud or prolonged call, but it quivers through the forest like a warm wind and is answered by the soft cluck of a female.

The gobbling is a relief. We have not seen a turkey for months. The previous winter they came regularly to scratch for seed below the bird feeders. I haven't seen them since early fall when the chicks had shed their fuzz in favour of a young-adult look. We worried about how many made it through the winter. Winter is a dangerous time for them, especially since we suspect a poacher has been at work in the back woodlot.

The worry evaporates when I walk through the back acreage and spot two large adult turkeys hiking across a ridge. Then two more, followed by another three, then another two. They march with straight, stiff legs and heads erect like a platoon of soldiers on patrol.

They are a big bird, the largest game bird in North America. They stand up to almost one metre tall. Males average eight kilograms in weight, females four kilograms. Like loons, they have a prehistoric look with their bluish-grey heads and wrinkled red throats. They appear dark brown in some light, but their feathers actually are much more colourful with light brown bands.

Diane sums up their appearance: "They are so homely that they are beautiful!"

The next day, I take my coffee cup to the front windows where I always start my day with a look out at paradise. There is a movement of brown below the feeders. The turkeys are back, three of them hunch-backed as their heads bob, snatching seed from the ground. When they feed they look like question marks that have fallen on their faces. The sun is shining on their backs bringing out the iridescent beauty in their feathers, first green, then bronze, and almost red.

I call Diane, who is thrilled to see that her friends have survived the dangers of winter: the foxes, coyotes, wolves, deep snow, bitter cold, and the poacher. Later we hear more encouraging news: someone farther up the road reports having seen as many as two dozen turkeys in the bush.

Diane was the first to discover that wild turkeys, pretty much wiped out in Ontario by early settlement, had taken up residence at St. Nora Lake. One day back in the late 1990s she asked if I had heard a gobbling in the woods behind the cottage.

"Gobbling? Like a turkey?" I asked.

She confirmed she thought she had heard a turkey gobbling. A day or two later she heard it again, and we all thought she had sipped some bad wine. We called the Ministry of Natural Resources. They confirmed there were no turkeys living this far north. The turkey restoration program was still young and the farthest north turkeys had been reported was Orillia. Another case proving that bureaucracy takes its time in catching up with reality.

The rebirth of the eastern wild turkey in Ontario is a wonderful success story. Turkeys were common in the southern half of the province before settlers cleared the forests, shrinking habitat. In 1984 the Ontario government started a restoration program, bringing in turkeys from the United States. They took root and now the Ontario turkey population is estimated at 70,000-plus.

Having the turkeys back is less cool on some April mornings just as dawn breaks. I am awakened by loud and urgent gobbling in the ravine behind the cottage. There is a Tom back there who insists on sending out his love calls during the best part of my sleep. He has wakened me on a couple of mornings so I decide it's payback time. I get up, grab my Quaker Boy "Screaming Green" hen call, and slip out onto the bedroom balcony. I give my best "Hey big boy, I'm over here" call.

He responds enthusiastically. I know he's moving out of the ravine. I peer around the corner of the cottage and see him coming. He's hot to trot, gobbling and strutting as he comes, and has two younger males, Jakes just starting to reach the Tom status, behind him. I guess they are coming to watch in hopes of picking up pointers.

He hits the knoll behind the cottage, looking around while I give a couple more sexy clucks. He's a dandy. A good twenty-pounder with a classic face: grey, blue, and bright red extending down his wattled neck. He is perplexed that he can't see the object of his love. He gobbles again, then fans his magnificent tail, hoping that the hen is hiding, will see his impressive wares, and come out to him.

No such luck. I giggle and leave the balcony to go back to bed. That'll teach him. He's standing there, unhappy and perplexed that the hen was not impressed by his calls and displays, and ran off with someone else.

He won't be upset too long. A dominant Tom like this one has a harem of up to ten females in his patch of bush. He'll gobble at any time of year but is most often heard during the spring mating season. He gobbles, pushes forward his breast, fans his huge tail feathers, drags his wings on the ground, and struts to attract the females.

The most insistent spring gobbling indicates that the ladies are not interested. When they do become interested later, you'll hear much less gobbling in the woods.

The females scratch depressions in the forest floor to build their nests. They lay one egg a day for up to three weeks. However, every morning they hear the gobbling and leave the nests to sneak out to the mating grounds. The average clutch is eleven eggs laid over two weeks. Incubation takes twenty-eight days. The chicks are hatched at the beginning of June and look like balls of dandelion fluff. They leave their egg shells running — well certainly soon after hatching — and start to fly after one or two weeks.

Not many more than 60 percent of the eggs hatch successfully. The little guys who do make it don't fare much better — roughly 50 percent die within a month.

One of the myths about wild turkeys is that they are endless wanderers, walking many kilometres every day. Actually, they seldom cover more than four kilometres in a day. Another misconception: not just the males have beards, the string of fine feathers that protrude from the chest and grow up to around thirty centimetres long. Up to 10 percent of females can have beards.

We are ecstatic about the turkeys, but worried about some of the other birds. We have not seen a blue jay in months. In the past when they haven't been around in a while we set out a handful of peanuts, and within minutes hear a "jayer-jayer" call, which is soon followed by a flash of lavender blue on darker blue trimmed in black and white.

The bold and aggressive jays are not the only birds missing this spring. Smaller birds are not coming in the large numbers of earlier years. The beautiful yellow grosbeaks that used to descend on our feeders have not shown in three years. Ditto the yellow finches. Even the chickadees are fewer in number.

The National Audubon Society in the U.S. reported in 2007 that there are only 5.2 million Boreal Chickadees in North America compared with 20 million in 1967. That's a drop of 73 percent. The grosbeaks are down 78 percent, from 17 million in 1967 to 3.8 million forty years later. Global warming, deforestation of winter ranges in the south, and constant human invasion everywhere are given as reasons for the declines.

Sketch by Zita Poling Moynan.

Advancing civilization has done some horrible things to wildlife. Thankfully, some good things are happening, like the successful reintroduction of the Eastern Wild Turkey. They are a joy to watch at our winter bird feeders.

Even our good works to restore the health of species sometimes are harmful. Take the case of the partridge, also known as the ruffed grouse. His chances for repopulation have been hurt by the successful attempts to restore wild turkey populations. Turkeys eat some of the things grouse do, and will raid grouse nests. The partridge also have been hurt by the expanding deer populations, which are over browsing many of our forests, leaving less to eat for other species.

The Audubon Society studies show the ruffed grouse has suffered a 54 percent population decline, down from fifteen million birds to 6.8 million over a forty-year period. Logging of their territories, larger deer populations and more northern goshawks, a natural predator, are reasons for the decline. I don't need Audubon statistics to tell me about the ruffed grouse. I have watched their numbers decline at St. Nora Lake for twenty years.

In our roughly seventy acres, I know for certain of only one partridge. Twenty-five years ago, this region was a partridge haven where you could see small flocks feeding together. Like most animals, the partridge populations follow cycles, but my observations are that there has not been a significant up cycle in more than a decade.

The one partridge I do know of soon will be out at the edge of the hardwoods looking for love. His drumming to attract females and scare off competitors is a throbbing that sounds like a motorboat off in the distance. He makes it by standing on a log and beating his wings furiously against the air. I hope he finds a mate and begins repopulating our woods.

During a walk through the woods I confirm he has made it through the winter. I surprise him sunning himself against an uprooted tree. He skitters away, body flattened, chin almost touching the earth in a comical effort to pretend that I can't see him.

These birds are the size of a small chicken and are sensational flyers, able to hover and turn quickly even in the thickest bush. In eastern Canada they have mottled grey and brown feathers, and dark brown neck feathers that are especially large in the males and form a ruff that rises and surrounds their heads when they are displaying for mating.

More good news this spring: the pileated woodpecker is back. We hear him hammering on a standing dead poplar behind the cottage. We sneak out and find him, a large Woody Woodpecker–type bird with red head battering the tree so hard that large chips are flying as if hit by a lumberman's axe. You can identify his work; large rectangular holes in the sides of trees. These exciting birds became scarce when the North American forests were cleared, but rebounded nicely in the last fifty years or so.

Each animal sound in the woods is wonderfully unique, but none matches the one that floats over the water as the ice leaves. It is the haunting signature sound of cottage country: the call of the arriving loons.

We haven't heard it this year. We are wondering why, but are not too worried. It's possible the loons have picked a back bay in which to nest this year. They never seem to go back to the same place, probably because they have a habit of nest building in the most unsuitable places. Once they put a nest at the edge of the rocky shore out front our place and the waves washed it away. Quite often they will build a nest at a waterfront site which even the dumbest fox can access easily to snatch the eggs or chicks.

It's not nice to slag the great icon of the north country. However, it must be said that these are not the brightest birds in bush country. They are beautiful — a beauty that is almost prehistoric. Their black heads are almost iridescent, made more striking by their piercing red eyes. The white necklace around the black neck and white spots on the black back and sides surely were placed by an unseen creator.

They are a big bird, 2.7 to 6.3 kilograms, heavy because their bones are solid, which allows them to make deep dives up to seventy metres for food. Most bird bones are hollow to allow for easier flight. Loons can stay under water for three minutes or more, but on average dive to five metres and stay under for roughly forty-five seconds.

There are an estimated 65,000 common loon pairs in Ontario alone. Their life expectancy is fifteen to thirty years. St. Nora usually has two pairs. One year they arrived when the ice was not fully out and took to fishing in the small open patches along the shorelines.

The loons are out there somewhere, and we expect to hear their joyous laughter on a quiet, moonlit night as we sit looking out over the lake. We'll smile when we hear them. We know their joy at being back is so great that they are laughing at the moonbeams dancing crazily on the lake.

Later in the spring we'll watch them fishing off the little island out front, their white and black checkered backs and wings glinting in the sun, the blood-red eyes ever alert in their coal black heads. If they have picked a reasonably safe spot to incubate their eggs and raise their young we will see them swimming in early summer with a chick or two perched on their backs.

We will see them. We know that, because they are a magic bird. Their yodels are hopeful calls telling us that if we try harder, we can do more to save our natural environment.

— 6 —
GIFTS OF SPRING

"To sit in the shade on a fine day and look upon verdure is the most perfect refreshment."
— Jane Austen

Sawing logs, swinging a splitting axe and stacking the woodpile brutalizes the back but stimulates the appetite. I'm fortunate to have married someone who not only knows how to cook, but who finds joy in planning, preparing, and presenting new and different dishes for different seasons. She also is way ahead of the curve in the trend to eat more food produced locally. So when spring dinner bells ring, I can expect something scrumptious from the surrounding woods and waters.

The absolute best spring meal is something that you can get fresh only in April: fried smelts and succulent new dandelion leaves. Roll the smelt in flour and bit of oil, add a touch of salt and fry them. The dandelions need only some oil and vinegar and a bit of salt for taste.

Freshwater smelt, for anyone not familiar with this northern delicacy, swim up rivers and creeks to spawn when the ice begins to leave the lakes. Shine a flashlight into a spawning stream at night in spring and you'll see thousands of silver bodies pushing against the current. They are a small fish, about twenty centimetres long.

Smelting is done mainly at night, with the thickest runs in the dark hours past midnight. Years ago that was not a problem. Now, for a body that yearns for sleep just as the ten o'clock news begins, smelting means setting an alarm clock.

It also means keeping a sharp eye when bringing the smelts back to the cottage. There's the dark walk out to the shed where the cleaning takes place, a walk that leaves a trail of fish odour that no night rambling bear could miss a kilometre away.

One recent year, not far from Shaman's Rock, a guy went out to check his shed and to see why the dog was barking. He was grabbed by a black bear and bitten on the arm. He escaped only by pounding a rock across the bear's snout.

Smelting isn't as popular as it once was when people in hip boots lined streams and dipped wire mesh nets to scoop the finger-length fish by the hundreds. Decades ago along streams like Thunder Bay's Current River, you could see dozens of smelters scooping smelt into the beds of pickup trucks. Nowadays we just take a bucket or can with small holes punched in it to scoop a couple dozen smelt just for a taste.

We heard during the spring of 2010 that up at Huntsville, a forty-minute drive north of our place, the smelt were running so thick that some people were scooping them from the water with their hands.

Dandelion leaves are not easy to get in cottage country. They need open spaces and do not favour the forests. However, like many other invaders from the city they have found little spots on which to grab a foothold. We prowl grassy spots near cottages, ruling out areas where dogs might go regularly or where someone might have used chemical fertilizers.

Dandelions are best when they are young and tender, just getting going after the snow slips away. We cut them out of the ground with a kitchen knife and wash them thoroughly several times. They taste like chicory or escarole, with a juicy sweetness that has a lightly flavoured bite. As they get larger they get tough and bitter. You can eat them then, but it's best to boil them.

Smelts, dandelion salad, and draft beer make the best cottage meal, and maybe because it happens only once a year.

The dessert to cap off a meal of smelts and dandelions is, of course, maple syrup, another gift of spring. Maple syrup making is a North American tradition that goes back to the Natives who tapped sugar maple trees and caught the dripping sap in bark vessels.

Like many other cottagers in hardwood country we have a few spigots and cans for collecting syrup during March when the nights are cold and the days are starting to warm. It's fun to collect a bit of maple sap and cook it into golden brown sweet syrup. No one gets much more than a taste. You need forty ounces of sap to reduce to one ounce of syrup. So you need to collect several buckets of sap just to get enough syrup for one family breakfast.

Down the highway from our lake, Big Jim Emes has run a maple syrup operation for many years. His sugar maple tree taps are connected to plastic lines that feed down to his sugar shack where the water in the syrup is reduced in a huge tin evaporator warmed by a wood fire.

Visiting a syrup operation in March is cool for kids. Years ago we took two of our grandchildren, Jessica and Robert, to see the Emes operation. Robert wanted to taste the liquid coming out of the trees so Big Jim, as tall as a maple and wearing his bushy grey beard, ladled out some uncooked sap to let him taste, but warned him not to taste too much. Robert gulped the works, then had diarrhea for the rest of the day.

One of the best maple syrup outings in our part of the country used to occur at the Leslie Frost Centre before it was closed by the provincial government. The Ministry of Natural Resources ran the place and in March had a little maple syrup weekend. A hay wagon took families to the old demonstration sawmill off Highway 35, then through the bush to a sugar shack where kids could watch how maple syrup is made in the sugar shack and eat maple taffy made from spreading fresh syrup on snow.

A biologist conducted tours through the bush telling the kids about the trees, how they are tapped, plus some thoughts on being environmentally conscious. Afterwards, the hay wagon took people back to the Frost Centre where they could have a breakfast of pancakes and maple syrup for a few bucks each.

The government closed the Frost Centre in 2004, ending a rich history in natural resources education. The bureaucrats and politicians said the place was losing money but the figures used to support that argument were suspicious. Politics closed the place. The riding was represented by an opposition politician. If the local political boss had been on the government side, the Frost Centre would be alive and thriving.

The Leslie Frost Centre provided a place for provincial law enforcement officers to receive training and other agencies to conduct seminars and workshops in a quiet, yet accessible setting where millions of dollars had been spent on upgrading accommodations and kitchen facilities. It now sits on St. Nora Lake empty and desolate, costing the government hundreds of thousands of dollars a year to maintain the place while it figures out what to do with it.

We miss the noise of excited school kids who used to be bused in from urban areas to learn the joys of life beyond the asphalt. I remember the little faces peering from the school bus windows, faces with eyes wide in wonder. I wonder where they go now to learn about smelts and dandelions and maple syrup and other pieces of outdoor heritage that once were an integral part of Canadian life?

If I won a lottery I would buy the Frost Centre and turn it into a place where under-privileged kids from the mean streets of Toronto could visit, enjoy, and learn about an environment that is more natural than the one in which they live. I see them walking on paths strewn with pine needles, not needles shed by drug addicts. I see them smelling a campfire burning sweet birch, instead of factory smoke and car exhaust. They would hear the calls of the loons instead of the crack of automatic pistols. They would learn that in nature every plant and animal has an important purpose, and how all parts of nature complement each other and respect each other.

The only good thing about the Frost Centre now that it is abandoned, is that it is a good place to go and search for spring dandelions.

— 7 —
FLY SEASON

"Do what we can, summer will have its flies."
— Ralph Waldo Emerson

The chainsaw is chucking out nice little chunks of oak — a sign of a well-sharpened chain — when the first hit happens. No warning, just a buzz inside my right ear. Blackfly! I straighten up to see a small cloud of them, unfocused and flying about disoriented. Newly hatched.

So, the season begins, and I ask myself once again why I can never seem to get the spring wood done before they come. It has been a long, dry, and gentle spring. The best one could hope for, yet I still haven't got all the outside work finished before the spring has ended.

In the cottage world, spring has ended when the flies appear. They seem to schedule their appearance with the leaves. When the leaves bud red on the maples and bright light green on the poplars, you know the flies are just over the next hill. When the new leaflets burst through their bud skins, the bugs appear. They can be fierce for two or three weeks, then taper until the start of July when they become tolerable.

Now that they are here I know I have a few days grace. They don't bite when they first come out, just fly about your head letting you know they are there, building an appetite. After a few days to a week, they get serious and it's time to get out the protection or stay inside.

The blackfly is our greatest spring curse. It is gnat-like and tiny, ranging in size from one to five millimetres, although I've never seen one that big and don't want to. There are more than 1,250 species in the world, some yellowish-orange, some brownish grey, but ours are black.

They lay their eggs in moving water, unlike mosquitoes, which do their hatching in still pools and puddles.

The good news about blackflies is that only the females bite. They have microscopic bladelike cutters in their mouths that saw through skin. These ladies use blood for development of their eggs. The really bad news is that researchers believe that there are times, depending on species and conditions, when blackflies will bite through strong repellents.

The bites produce red lumps that are insanely itchy. The best chances of avoiding bites is to wear light-coloured clothing and to skip shaving lotions and deodorants. Blackflies are mainly attracted to carbon dioxide from breath and perspiration, so there's not much you can do about that except to wear repellents and netting. No insect is more adept at getting under collars, inside waistbands, hat bands, boot tops, and sleeves.

There are truckloads of boastful claims about repellents, almost all of which are nonsense. Here's my experience: there is only one effective fly repellent and it is spelled DEET (for N,N-diethyl-meta-toluamide). The heavier the concentration the better, which is difficult these days because of concerns that DEET can cause human health problems. Lots of things cause human health problems, so I keep in my bug jacket pocket a small bottle of 97 percent DEET bought in backwoods North Carolina.

My governments tell me that lower concentrations of DEET are just as effective. However, my governments tell me many things that I do not believe. The Ontario government does have an informative piece on DEET, reasonably free of mind-numbing bureaucratese, at *http://health.gov.on.ca/ en/public/programs/publichealth/wnv/default.aspx/wnv_mn.html.*

Blackflies love shaded areas and are most fiercely aggressive in the deeper woods where there is little sunlight. Hot sunlight in open areas around the cottage keeps them at bay. The best news is that blackflies do not bite indoors and are not out and about too often after dark.

The most widespread myth about blackflies in cottage country is that they pollinate the blueberry bushes. You'll hear people rationalizing the existence of these pests with: "Well, the more there are, the better the blueberries." Blackflies do not pollinate blueberry bushes. That's straight from the folks at the National Research Council. They do, however, suck nectar from blueberry flowers, fuel that helps them fly about to terrorize innocent cottagers.

Spring's public enemy no. 2 is the mosquito, until the blackflies begin to die off. Then it becomes no. 1. It is among the world's most fascinating and most deadly insects. Much has been written about the mosquito, but probably the best book ever on the bug is *Mosquito: The Story of Man's Deadliest Foe*. The book is scientific but highly readable, a tribute to the interesting combination of authors: Andrew Spielman, a top insect scientist, and Michael D'Antonio, a fine writer and reporter.

Exquisite in design, almost as light as air, these dusty-brown vampire ballerinas are mankind's greatest enemy. They hatch billions of newborns every day around the world. They kill almost one million humans per year, many of them children, by spreading serious diseases such as malaria and dengue fever. As with blackflies, mosquitoes use animal blood for egg production and feed on plant juices for energy. Hundreds of thousands of mosquitoes are born every day in cottage country, but thankfully their life span is only two weeks. However, in those two weeks, they are breeding new generations so the mosquito crop is with us until at least late summer. Mosquitoes start mating when they are two days old.

Mosquitoes have been an intolerable nuisance to northern cottagers, but never a serious health threat until recent years. Malaria, dengue fever, yellow fever, and various other deadly mosquito-borne fevers thankfully do not exist in our cottage lands. The arrival of West Nile virus has made the mosquito more than an irritant, however.

West Nile first appeared in New York State in 1999 and by the summer of 2001 was found in birds and mosquitoes in Southern Ontario. The U.S. Centres for Disease Control and Prevention (CDC) tracked sixty-six cases in New York that first year, with seven deaths. In 2009, the CDC reported 722 cases and eighteen deaths.

In Canada, forty-two humans died from the virus and its complications between 2002 and 2009. However, human cases of West Nile rise and dive depending on the year. For instance, there were 2,200 cases reported in Canada in 2007, but only eight human cases, none fatal, in 2009.

Birds, notably crows, carry the virus. Mosquitoes take blood from birds, just as they do from humans. The bugs become West Nile carriers when they bite an infected bird. If that mosquito bites you, she likely will pass along the virus. If you begin noticing dead birds in an area, that can be a sign that West Nile is present.

Some people have had West Nile from a mosquito bite but did not realize it. Often the symptoms are mild, with a fever, headache, and body aches. However, West Nile can be severe, causing high fever, stiff neck, disorientation, convulsions, paralysis, and death.

The chances of being bitten by an infected mosquito are quite small. Researchers estimate that fewer than 1 percent of mosquitoes in a given area are infected. The chances that one infected mosquito in your area will bite you are very low.

However, complacency is one of the dangers of this new West Nile threat. At Shaman's Rock we have to remind ourselves to follow all the steps for avoiding mosquito bites, especially for the children. There is a chance that just one bite could cause a tragedy. We stress putting a lotion repellent on the kids, wearing light-coloured clothing, and staying away from dark, dank places that mosquitoes love.

The encouraging news about mosquitoes is that they seldom travel farther than one hundred metres from their birthplace. Which means cottagers should be diligent about searching out and dumping sources of stagnant water around the cottage: cans, containers, old tires, and anything else that will hold small amounts of water that mosquitoes will find for laying eggs. If you use a rain barrel, screen the top of it.

Mosquitoes, unlike blackflies, love to be indoors, especially at night. Probably nothing is more irritating than that lone mosquito buzzing around your ear at three o'clock in the morning. Burning mosquito coils really knocks down mosquitoes indoors, but they also carry health concerns. A least one serious study shows that coils give off pollutants similar to cigarette smoke, including cancer-causing elements.

We've never tried the zappers that some people put out on their decks or in their yards to fry mosquitoes. Various research projects have cast doubt on their effectiveness, but some folks praise them.

Of course, when the blackflies and mosquitoes start to thin out, in come the horse flies and deer flies. They are the bigger beasts that dive-bomb your head while you are swimming in the lake or walking in the woods. Repellent will not keep them away, but will stop them from biting.

The happiest moment in bug season is the arrival of the air cavalry. You don't hear the slap of the wing rotors but you see them banking and diving. It's the dragonflies. When they hatch, they lift off and comb the airways around the cottage, gulping down thousands of flies caught unawares.

The arrival of the dragonfly cavalry reminds me of that great scene in the movie *Apocalypse Now* when Lieutenant Colonel Bill Kilgore (Robert Duvall) is standing in front of the helicopter squadron taking off for a mission in Vietnam. He looks out at the scene and says: "I love the smell of napalm in the morning."

When the dragonflies come out, I stand out on the deck, wave my U.S. cavalry hat, and shout: "Go get'um guys!"

I love the sight of dragonflies feeding in the morning.

— 8 —
ALL CRITTERS GREAT AND SMALL

"All animals are equal but some animals are
more equal than others."
— GEORGE ORWELL, *ANIMAL FARM*

I confess that I have done bad things to little creatures. You don't have to dig too deep anywhere around Shaman's Rock to unearth the bones of small critters that I have dispatched in defence of my property. I know it was wrong, but I plead self defence and/or insanity.

The Shaman's Rock Wars against little creatures broke out soon after I began building my dream. No sooner had the first pieces of lumber been banged together than they arrived. Mice by the dozens, drawn by the odours of free food. Then, red squirrels. Red squirrels in herds, some looking for a warm place to winter, but many coming as part of a plan to irritate me until I would run away screaming through the bush.

Flying squirrels chewed their way into the cottage eaves. I found and plugged their entrance. Weeks later they were still coming and going at night, raising hell behind the walls, but leaving no trace of how they were entering and exiting. I called an exterminator. Two guys crawled all over the building. After an hour they came down scratching their heads, charged me seventy-five bucks, and said it was a mystery to them.

The mystery ended when flying squirrels chewed through an inside wall and were trapped in the cottage for two weeks. They died of thirst, one curling up on a bed pillow to expire.

I guess to be reasonable, it is their country and I could have been more understanding of their need to invade my private space. However, gnawed woodwork, pee stains on the new insulation, mice poop on the kitchen counter, and little feet drumming on the walls during the night made me completely unreasonable.

What knocked me over the edge was the squirrel takeover of my bunkhouse. I had dreamed of creating a writing retreat there. Unfortunately, when I built it I neglected to put heavy wire screening under the roof vent. Red squirrels chewed the light mesh I had installed, moved in, and started to party. They were followed soon by their cousins, the flying squirrels, and battalions of mice. The parties went on non-stop and they trashed the place.

I mounted a restoration campaign that involved replacing part of the roof and stripping the inside walls to the studs. I was not amused, and neither was my bank account.

When the flies are out in serious numbers, no one is amused as we race to get the bug tent up on the deck. We flail at the air, slap behind our ears, dance and scream as we throw the frame poles together, then throw the tenting over the frame. Job done, we feel safe and sit to gather ourselves. Then we see them. Twelve to fourteen holes of various sizes in the screen walls. The mice exacted their revenge on us during the winter, spitefully chewing holes in the mesh.

All cottages have mice at one time or another. They are creepy critters and can be dangerous if they are carrying the Hantavirus that can be spread to humans. The virus is in the saliva, urine, and droppings of deer mice and other rodents. It can infect people who breathe in dust and tiny particles that float in the air, especially when sweeping out mice-infested areas. It causes severe pulmonary problems, even death.

Cottagers should not sweep or vacuum mice nests or droppings. Opening windows and doors before cleaning up such messes is a good idea. So is wearing rubber gloves and using disinfectant on traps.

Hantavirus or not, mice certainly can scare guests.

In the days when the inside walls of Shaman's Rock were still yellow insulation covered with plastic, many a guest awakened to see mice scampering along the inside of the plastic. That was always good for a few screams in the night.

Contraptions for catching mice or driving them off are as numerous as the mice. Most do not work, or work with extreme complications. Traps often catch more fingers than mice and present the problems of body removal and disposal. There are poisons, which are not a good idea with kids and pets about. Also, poisoned mice have a penchant for running off and hiding in walls to rot, filling the entire cottage with the odour of death.

Then there are the glue sheets. These are paper sheets covered with a sticky substance and are placed in areas where mice travel. They are a good idea until the day you check the traps and find a mouse with his feet stuck on the paper. There he is, desperately trying to lift his feet while staring at you with excruciatingly sad eyes.

If you are going to use traps, buy good ones. I like the Victor brand traps, and the ones with the yellow plastic trip plate that give off the smell of cheese.

Even good traps are problematic, however, and mankind has worked for centuries to build a better mouse trap. One day it hit me that the better mouse trap had been invented. I just had forgotten about it.

I had a boyhood friend whose dad was boss of a logging camp east of Thunder Bay, then Port Arthur and Fort William. On school vacations, my friend would return home to the Black Sturgeon area bush and would sometimes bring me along. We had the run of the camp and learned much, including a neat way of trapping mice. The camp cooks used to deal with the mice by setting up a bucket half filled with water. They drilled a hole on each side of the bucket rim and inserted a piece of wooden dowel. The underside of the dowel was dabbed with peanut butter or cream cheese. The mice walked the dowel and when they bent their heads to lick the bait, the dowel would roll and they would tumble into the water and drown. Back in those days, lumberjacks still walked floating logs and wore cork-soled or spiked boots to keep them from slipping off. Some bright logger likely used his log walking experiences in designing the mouse bucket trick.

I built a mice bucket from memory and it worked like a charm. I placed it in a dugout room under the cottage and soon had buckets of mice. Eventually all signs of mice in and around the cottage disappeared. The bucket obviously works well but I must give credit also to a furry little friend who found warmth and comfort by digging a route into the lower pump room.

My wild friend is a pine marten. A vicious little fellow with long, razor-sharp teeth. He doesn't bother me, I don't bother him. He does eat mice so he's welcome to live in the pump room, as long as he doesn't get excited when I have to go down there.

The war against squirrels has been complicated. The mouse-in-a-bucket weapon was of no use against the squirrels. They are much too clever. I quickly learned that a dose of lead produced the best results. I started with a BB gun, moved up to a pellet gun, and finally, when I realized I was losing the battle, moved up to a full choke shotgun. I think that was after I discovered that a red squirrel had chewed a hole in the gasoline tank of my brand new ATV, costing me a couple hundred bucks.

I had lost all perspective. I had become a deranged killer, but it was not all my fault. I was under volcanic pressures. Diane yelled at me to keep them away from her bird feeders. My neighbour Doug Fraser offered me bounties after he discovered a family of red squirrels living in his sock drawer.

Bills for shotgun shells were mounting up, yet the squirrel population was not diminishing. One day I dispatched two at the bird feeders and when I was leaving the cottage after a weekend, I saw two more sitting on a rock at the end of the driveway. I think they were waving, and I saw both were wearing taunting, evil grins.

A monstrous exaggeration, you say? Well, consider the Associated Press story from March 2011: "A Vermont neighbourhood is being stalked by a renegade grey squirrel. Several people in Bennington say they've been attacked by a squirrel over the last few weeks." One guy was shovelling snow when the squirrel jumped on him and viciously attacked him. Imagine, minding his own business, shovelling snow. Full proof of the terrorist tactics these creatures will apply against cottagers, and others.

I tried various strategies to keep the squirrels out of the bird feeders. Thin wire line that the squirrels could not walk. The line broke. Sheet metal baffles to keep them from climbing trees and jumping onto the feeders. They found routes around them. Nothing worked. Finally an animal-loving friend suggested I simply let the squirrels feed from the feeders. I couldn't do that. It was expensive and the squirrels would never leave any seed for the birds.

I compromised. I began spilling a bit of seed on the ground under the feeders. We could make a deal: squirrels stay out of the feeders, my shotgun stays in the closet. So far it has been a happy truce that has allowed me to concentrate on problems created by bigger game: raccoons and bears.

Raccoons are cute nuisances. They usually won't come around unless they pick up an intriguing odour, food left about, or a garbage bag not securely tucked away. The worse thing they have ever done at Shaman's Rock is shriek like banshees at each other in middle-of-the-night fights over the freshest addition to compost heap.

Sketch by Zita Poling Moynan.

The Ojibwe called racoons *arakun*, which means "he who scratches with his hand." They will use their hands to hold a rock for smashing clams.

Their signature black masks are not the only feature that identifies them as clever thieves of the night. They have hairless little hands that they manipulate with a dexterity that is amazing for a forest animal. The Algonquian Indians called them "arakun," which means "he scratches with his hand." There are stories that raccoons can use tools with their hands, like smashing a rock against a clam to break its shell.

Raccoons were quick to get into our bird feeders and we had to engineer baffles to keep them from getting into the tree and down onto the feeders. They were winning that battle, until I bought a live trap.

One particularly bad offender became my favourite seed thief because he had a distinct personality. He was bold and clever, figuring out how to get tasty bait from the cage trap without setting off the trip plate that brings down the trap door. I watched him carefully lift a front foot over the trip plate, then another. He kept his belly tucked in while he grabbed the bait and just as carefully backed out of the trap. He had it figured that if any part of his body pressed on the plate, there would be a clang and his exit would be sealed. He learned this after being trapped several times.

The first time I trapped him I hiked him back into the woods and released him. A couple of days later, Diane saw a raccoon at a bird feeder.

"That's the guy you caught and brought into the back bush," she said.

"Impossible," I said. "He was so terrified, he'd never come back."

A few nights later, I trapped another raccoon, which looked quite familiar. This time I put him in the back of the truck and drove a couple kilometres down the highway to release him.

"He's back," said Diane a few days later.

I watched him in the feeder and had to admit he did look like the same raccoon I had trapped a couple of times. I trapped him yet again and this time loaded him into the tin boat and dropped him into the wilderness across the lake.

"You won't believe it," said Diane a week later. "It's Hector." We had become so used to having him around that we gave him a name.

"No way," I said. "He would have to walk forty kilometres around the lake, or swim right across it."

We got him again and this time decided to mark him. I spray-painted his fluffy tail with fluorescent orange paint, and boated him across to the far shore. Within a week I noticed a determined-looking raccoon trying to get into a garbage can. He had an orange tail!

His persistence impressed me, but I was perplexed on how to get rid of him. That's when he started getting in and out of the trap without getting caught. I experimented, did some modifications, and trapped him again and this time drove him to a garbage dump on the far side of Dorset. I watched as he slowly emerged from the trap, then gave him a little boot tap on the bum while yelling: "You want garbage. Here's garbage. Go crazy for the rest of your life."

The guy who manages the dump gave me a strange look. I never saw Hector again.

I have yet to put my boot to the behind of a nuisance bear. I have yelled at a couple from the safety of the cottage. I also have thrown a rock at one that was making off with a grandson's soccer ball. What a bear planned to do with a soccer ball, I have no idea. I was just thrilled it was a ball and not the kid.

Bears are moody and unpredictable. They also are sneaky and silent. They aren't called the Black Ghosts of the Forests for nothing. Silent they might be, but I can hear one twenty metres away in the dark of the night.

Champion sleeper that I am, I am bolt upright in bed when I hear one step on a branch or brush a tree as it approaches our bird feeders at four o'clock in the morning. Thunderstorms do no wake me, but bears in the bird feeders do.

Years pass without a hint of bear at Shaman's Rock. Then suddenly, bears everywhere, every night. Once they find a worthwhile snack at your place, they will come back regularly to see what else there is.

Our latest bear outbreak began because of composting. I mean how tasty is a leaf of wet decaying lettuce and the stem end of a tomato? Plenty, I guess, because we had a bear that trashed our composting container every night for a week. When we took the composter away, it began tearing down all the bird feeders.

Later, a younger bear came and stole a food cooler off the deck. It was a soft-cover cooler on wheels and was packed with hors d'oeuvres our daughter Leanna had prepared for a family gathering. No one had seen or heard anything, but when the daughter went to get the hors d'oeuvres the cooler was missing. A search was mounted, without finding a trace.

"Bear got it," I said.

Everyone ignored me. No one was ready to believe that a bear had come up on the front deck and grabbed a cooler sitting beside the front doors. I'm used to being ignored in such situations so I quietly went to the gun locker, pulled out my 7-30 Waters and slipped unnoticed into the woods.

I found the bear two ridges back snacking greedily on the hors d'oeuvres. He scented me but took an extra couple of last gulps before bolting. He was just getting into the red pepper dip when I interrupted him. He already had eaten seventy-five jalapeño poppers. It would be easy to track him now. I'd just follow the belching and the trail of bowel gas, but I decided maybe he had already learned a lesson.

Jaws dropped when I returned to the cottage, rifle in one hand, torn and tooth-marked cooler in the other.

That bear must have digested the jalapeño poppers without a problem because he returned the next night. We watched him as he grabbed a hard plastic cooler on the deck and started to toss the beer bottles out of it. That's when I put two shots over his head and sent him on his way. He didn't return.

It was our fault for leaving stuff out on the deck. However, we have had bears that were a serious nuisance even after we've taken down the bird feeders, stopped composting, and have been diligent about not leaving any food scraps or even odours outside.

Some people say there are more bears since the Ontario government cancelled the spring bear hunt some years back. All I know is that one in a half-dozen bears who might visit your place will become a genuine nuisance, and possibly a danger.

The provincial government tells us to report nuisance bears and it will deal with them. This is a huge amusement. The Ministry of Natural Resources' first response is "wait a couple weeks and maybe it will go away." The second response is "take down your bird feeders." That's good advice, but not much fun for all the people who love feeding and watching the birds.

The ministry, unofficially, would rather you handle a nuisance bear yourself. Some people deal with the matter with "extreme prejudice," a euphemism for .30-.30 Winchester, or similar high-powered solution. However, you must get ministry permission to shoot a bear, and must prove it is a danger or seriously destroying property. In cottage country, folks with a serious bear problem, and no time for the bureaucracy, follow the Three S Rule: Shoot. Shovel. Shut Up.

We have not shot a bear at Shaman's Rock, and hope we won't have to. It's not as simple as just aiming and pulling the trigger. You have to be guaranteed where the bullet is going. There are rocks for ricochets, branches for deflections. Shooting a bear usually involves a high-powered rifle, the slug from which can travel hundreds of metres. Shooting at anything around the cottage is just not a good idea unless the situation is desperate.

Most times bear problems disappear, and I hope that will always be the case, but I never rule out the Three S Rule. Bears are only Walt Disney cute from a far distance. They are dangerous wild animals and should be treated as such when necessary, and that is proven tragically true every year.

I was fishing in Algonquin Park one weekend many years ago when three young boys from the Pembroke area were stalked and killed by a black bear at Radiant Lake. They had been trout fishing and had stuffed their catches in their pockets.

More recently, Gerald Marois, forty-seven, of Waubaushene near Orillia, was charged by a big black bear while he was scouting the woods for the fall hunting season. The bear chased him into a tree but was able to reach his feet and legs. He chewed off Marois' boots, and ate part of his calf before knocking him out of the tree and inexplicably running away.

I laughed when I heard an MNR employee explain to the media that the bear mistook Marois for a deer. Mr. Marois also thought that was humorous, after the pain from his claw and bite wounds began to subside.

"He didn't mistake me for nothing," he told the *Toronto Star*. "That bear wanted to maul me; he was hungry and he came to get me."

Bears are a fact of life in cottage country, and appear to be growing in numbers. The best way to deal with them is start by learning more about them and viewing them with caution and respect, not outright fear. A good place on the Internet to learn about, and view bears on webcam, is the web page of the North American Bear Centre in Ely, Minnesota, at *www.bear.org*.

Bears, raccoons, squirrels, and mice. They can be damnable pests sometimes but I keep telling myself to put things in perspective. It's their country. They were here first. Respect their ways, and live as neighbours, even though they don't pay taxes like we do.

THERMOCLINE

— 9 —
SUNSHINE, SOUNDS, AND GUESTS

"I can enjoy society in a room; but out of doors,
nature is company enough for me."
— WILLIAM HAZLITT, *NEW MONTHLY MAGAZINE*, 1822

I am in the woods checking my domain when I hear the distant drone. I cock my head to follow its progress. Its path toward me is steady, and soon I am able to confirm the engine sound as one I know well. I hear it approach the treetops, then the pitch changes as the pilot banks over the lake for a pre-landing visual check.

It is Charlie Bravo India Zulu, C-BIZ, the white and red Super Cub two-seater built and flown by my friend and cottage neighbour Brian Bissell of Sarnia. He has the cottage three doors down and brings C-BIZ up for the summer. It is amphibious, with wheels in its floats, so he rolls it out of its hangar at Sarnia's Chris Hadfield Airport, lifts off from the black-top runway, and two hours later is floating on the lakefront at the cottage. This is really cool.

Brian is a mechanical genius who can figure out anything. He built C-BIZ himself, recently installed a new engine, put on the amfibs himself, and now has installed an auto-pilot. He even designed and built an aluminum lift system that cradles C-BIZ above the water line, protecting it from strong waves.

Most evenings he takes C-BIZ up to look for moose browsing in the swamps. Sometimes I tag along. I've been on longer jaunts with him, and as a wheels-only pilot I am overwhelmed by the freedom of float flying. In a country speckled with lakes and rivers, places to land and explore are beyond imagination.

Some cottagers don't appreciate an airplane's roar because they say it breaks into their quiet seclusion. I never hear it without feeling excitement in my chest, or stepping out onto the deck to watch one come or go. Some people, who have watched thousands of takeoffs and landings, and have performed hundreds or more themselves, never lose the thrill of seeing an airplane lift off or land. There is something mystical and holy about that moment when an aircraft cuts the bonds with earth. John McGee Jr., American aviator and poet killed in a plane crash in 1941, best described the moment in the poem *High Flight*:

> Oh I Have Slipped
> The Surly Bonds of Earth ...
> Put Out My Hand
> And Touched the Face of God

The roar of C-BIZ's rotary engine is but one of the cacophony of sounds that announce the official arrival of summer at the lake. Hammering echoes in the distance. Circular saws and chainsaws whine. Someone down the shore is running a weed whacker to knock down fast-growing underbrush. Joining all this is the *thunk, thunk, thunk* of the pileated woodpecker knocking the bark off a dead tree in search of bugs to eat.

Vehicle doors slam, announcing the arrival of vans that spill out excited children, dogs, and mountains of amusements like croquet sets and water toys. First to spill out are the most dreaded of cottage guests: the granddogs. Huge, shedding granddogs tossing off enough hair to spin scarves for one hundred winter carollers, and truly grand in their bowel movements.

Next come the legions of little people, arriving breathlessly beside my hammock to announce, "C'mon, it's time to go fishing!"

The arrival of the vans also triggers a sudden rush to grab the best seats at the waterfront. This is high season for the cottage guest, whose sole purpose when arriving here is to loaf. My sole purpose is to get some work out of them; extra hands for that long job list that requires more than one pair of hands.

One regular guest was my old newshound pal Ian Donaldson, who was willingly coerced into helping me hunt and drag firewood logs out of the forest. I would play hard on his fondness for beer and campfires, never missing an opportunity to impress upon him the joy of sitting around a campfire surrounded by good wood and even better beer.

Not all cottage guests are as compliant and understanding as was Ian. For instance, we had quite a time trying to calm the hysterical guest who found Mr. Twister, one of the granddog's rubber spider toys, inside her bed clothes.

The worst time for any guest at Shaman's Rock always was what we used to call Screaming Saturday, that spring nightmare day when we reconnected the water system and put in the docks.

Foot valve checked, and repaired as necessary, the black ABS water line had to be dragged into the lake, sunk, and weighted down. Then the horrors really began. Priming the old jet pump under the cottage, trying to clear air locks. Priming and cursing. Cursing and priming and coaxing until all the air left and water started flowing into the pressure tank.

Not many guests who participated in a Screaming Saturday ever returned. After a decade of Screaming Saturdays, we installed a heated water line with a pump in the lake, eliminating the annual line in, line out routine. Now all that's left of Screaming Saturdays is towing the docks from storage, then trying to bolt them together with wet, frozen fingers while the lake rolls and smirks.

The older the cottage guest, the more wily they are about being Shanghaied into a cottage work project. So years back I tended to snare the younger guests, especially those with an interest in our daughters.

I enlisted one young suitor to help me put in the water line one spring. He volunteered to swim out to set the water line foot valve in place. I rowed out in the boat and prepared a weight and marker float for the line. He was treading water patiently beside the boat when I absent-mindedly handed him a twelve-inch concrete block to be used as the weight. When I turned to hand him something else, he wasn't there. Only the screams from the dock alerted me to the fact that he had gone down with the block. We got the water line in and him out of the water, but I never saw him at the cottage again.

Shirkers and granddogs aside, summer is treasured family time. It is time away from the daily stresses of family life, a time to put things in perspective, to strengthen the bonds of families distanced by geography and different lives. Brothers and sisters see each other in a more relaxed light. Cousins get to know each other better by sharing the experiences of diving from the dock, exploring the woods, and catching fascinating bugs.

Extensions to the dining table are brought out, dusted, and set in place. Meals are like the old days when everyone squeezed into spots at the table and shared favourite foods, news of what is happening in their lives, and memories of times gone by. Blackberries and iPhones are turned off and put away.

A couple of years ago our oldest daughter, Marcella, gathered broken birch twigs and sat at table playing with them. Later in the day I looked up on the cottage wall to see the word FAMILY spelled out in birch twigs.

One six-letter word in twigs says all there is to say about cottages and summer.

— 10 —
ROAD WORK

"Nature, to be commanded, must be obeyed."
— Francis Bacon

Another sweet sound of early summer begins as a far off vibration, then a hum. It evolves into a low rumble, much like thunder beyond the horizon, and as it moves inland from the highway it is punctuated by an agonized grinding and the clang of metal striking stone. By the time it climbs the hill and turns the corner that leads into my slice of heaven, it is a cacophony of roaring and banging.

I watch it emerge from a wispy morning mist mixed with road dust, a horrid mechanical invasion into the cottage country solitude. It is a homely machine, yellow and acned with brown rust; a rapacious monster insect scraping and chewing the road with its steel lower mandible. It rolls forward tenaciously on four waist-high tires at its rear and two on its front, creating a back-to-front narrowing that makes the thing look even more insect-like.

Visible behind the glass eyes of this creature is a heavyset man who seems too large for the small control cab. He is wearing a company baseball cap and a fluorescent orange work shirt monogrammed *Tom Sr.* His large hands, weathered and hard, play a row of black control knobs so deftly that he reminds me of the organ master at a famous cathedral. A touch to one knob and the machine's blade digs deeper into the road. A push on another and the scraped up gravel is smoothed neatly beside the ditch.

Tom Prentice Sr. has arrived with his Fiat-Allis road grader and everyone is happy to see him. The annual spring grading grinds away washboard that sets molars chattering and fills gaping potholes that jolt your body from backside to brain. When he's finished playing his tune on the control panel, our road is wider and neatly ditched and as smooth as a freshly ironed baby blanket.

Tom Sr. is the patriarch of Tom Prentice and Sons of Minden, a company that excavates, hauls gravel and earth, installs septic tanks, restores shorelines, and does a variety of other heavy-duty cottage projects. But it's probably best known for road grading because it maintains dozens of cottage roads and has contracts to grade road shoulders for hundreds of kilometres of Ontario government highways and county roads. The sons in the company name are four: Jack, Tom, Tony, and Terry and all work in the business.

Like many cottage roads ours is owned by the cottagers because it runs through individual properties, and in some cases quite close to the cottages themselves. Some people want it to be like a super highway, others want it left narrow and rough to discourage speeding and unwanted extra traffic.

Tom Prentice does more than grade and maintain the road. He is a diplomat who can help bridge the differences of opinion over how the cottage road should be kept. Tom knows all the different feelings cottagers have about roads and is skilful at navigating compromises.

"I could be fighting every day of the week," Tom told me for a cottage road story I was writing for *Cottage Life* magazine. Differing opinions, different personalities ensure that there will be regular confrontations over cottage road maintenance.

Tom once crested a cottage road hill in his grader to find a tipsy lady in a housecoat blocking passage. She had built a barricade of gas cans and a hockey stick and roared that no one was going to clean her ditches or widen her road.

The one-kilometre road into Shaman's Rock is a mere laneway that serves twenty-seven cottages on the west shore of St. Nora Lake. It was strictly a summer track until the late 1980s. The snow did not leave it before mid-April or later, then another week or two was needed for it to dry up. The first passages over it in the spring provided anxious moments. You never knew when a wheel would sink into a soft spot.

We put up a "Road Closed" barrier each spring to stop anyone from driving over it while it was still shedding its frost. Some folks didn't want to wait, however, and this caused some hot words about rutting up the road.

Back in those days, cottagers arrived for the Queen's birthday weekend, also known as May 24th weekend, or the May Two-Four weekend, a nickname based on the cases of twenty-four beer traditionally lugged into the cottage with the groceries. That was when cottages were, well, cottages. Summer cottages intended for use from mid-May until Labour Day.

They were built with two-by-four stud construction, with single pane glass, and little or no insulation. They were closed up tight, often shuttered, long before the snow began to fall. Their occupants trekked back to towns and cities a day or two before school resumed, and few returned before the May Two-Four weekend.

Things have changed. Our more affluent society with flex working hours, electronic networking, snowmobiles, all-terrain vehicles, and more recreation time have turned cottaging into a four-season experience.

A trend to earlier retirement has seen many people sell out the expensive homes in the noisy city and move full time to the cottage. Brad Robinson, owner of Robinson's General Store in Dorset, has lived in cottage country all his life and says the biggest increase in the off season cottage population has been retired folks.

More demanding building codes and more high-tech building materials now mean many cottages are more like homes.

You now find cottagers on their nests any day of the week, any month of the year. Gone are those brief blocks of weekday solitude and silent winter weekends when you could sneak a day or two off work and head for the cottage in little traffic and arrive to find no one for kilometres around.

Year-round use means taking better care of the cottage road. That's where Tom comes in. He and his boys replace rotting culverts, clean the ditches to prevent washouts, and add gravel that over time disappears with the wind, water, and vehicle traffic.

We used to organize summer work parties to do our own road maintenance. We would repair washouts with picks and shovels, rake rough spots, and cut and haul away brush overgrowing the road edges. Over the years we discovered that throwing one hundred bucks each into an annual maintenance fund was a lot easier on aging backs.

In the beginning we were all enthusiastic and energy charged. We walked into Shaman's Rock over the snowmobile track. Later, as more snowmobiles packed the track, we ran a four-wheel drive truck in. That was always exciting, sweating about slipping off the packed track. We did more than once, which meant a couple hours of hard shovelling to get the truck back up on the track.

We were so keen that when we were building the cottage, we couldn't wait for the road to open in April or May. We didn't want to upset anyone by ignoring the "Road Closed" sign and driving in and damaging the soft road. So we hauled building materials on toboggans, or our backs. Not many cottagers will walk a spring road empty handed.

One time, about two o'clock in the morning, I walked the road in leather dress shoes and a tuxedo. It had been a hard few weeks at work and I couldn't stand the city any longer. So following our company's annual meeting and dinner, I drove up and hiked in without bothering to change.

Another night following an ice storm we walked in with two young grandchildren. The road, hilly and winding, was treacherous with a slick covering of frozen rain. Topping the little hill behind our cottage, Diane slipped and fell. We watched in amazement as she swooshed down the hill, past the cottage, and around the bend near the lake. She simply slid off into the blackness. The kids were wide-eyed and one exclaimed as Diane disappeared into the darkness: "There goes Nana!"

Many night trips were made along the winter and spring road. Like most cottagers, we were always hyper to get to lake, leaving Fridays after work, most often cooking supper at midnight while waiting for the place to warm up. It amazed me how Diane could cook such wonderfully diverse meals such as pasta primavera so late at night in a cold cottage. Hot dogs were never an option with her.

Our litigious society has changed a traditionally casual approach to cottage roads. These days if someone trespasses on your cottage road, trips on a loose piece of gravel, and breaks a leg, the courts sure enough will award him or her damages. Each cottager on the road will be liable for a share of the payout. At our place, we throw twenty-five bucks a year each into the pot and buy liability coverage for the road.

We all pay the same amount for maintenance fees and insurance. It didn't used to be that way. There were years of debate over whether folks at the front of the road should pay less because they use less road. Finally the lights came on in everyone's head and we went to an equal-billing system, which has provided us with safe, basically headache-free road still rough and narrow enough to discourage some people who perhaps don't belong there.

The Federation of Ontario Cottagers' Associations reported in 2011 that it conducted a survey that showed that 70 percent of its association members carry road liability insurance. The survey also showed that 90 percent of cottage roads are gravel, nearly all of them dead ends.

I miss the old road days. It's not quite the same driving up to the back door without any adventure. There are so many great memories of bridging washouts, emergency repairs by volunteers, brushing parties, night passages on foot during wild winter nights. There's some adventure in keeping it plowed out — we use a combination of contracted plowing and our own ATVs with plows — but that doesn't provide the same sense of pioneer spirit that we felt in the old days.

The mind loves to think back on all that stuff, but the body is glad to have it gone. I mean it's not that there is no other work to do at the cottage, especially during the spring transition.

— 11 —
THE PICTURE WALL

"Memory is a way of holding onto the things you …
never want to lose."
— FROM THE TELEVISION SHOW *THE WONDER YEARS*

I stand in the hallway studying the faces on the wall and hearing their voices. They are cottage voices from years now passed. Children laughing and splashing in the lake. Grand boys going up the hill to play in the tree house. Granddaughter Jessica and her teenage girlfriends giggling as they share secrets down in the bunkhouse.

The hallway is a memory lane with its wall of photos recording a quarter of a century of cottaging at Shaman's Rock. The photos speak to me about gatherings of family and friends, an excited child's first fish, dogs frolicking in the summer sunlight, and other special moments. I'm glad these special memories are captured on the wall. Most people who pass down the hallway pause to reflect on them. This is good because many of the things that have happened here are worth remembering.

There is the framed newspaper mock up celebrating our twenty-fifth wedding anniversary. That is really cool, especially because it shows how much has changed in our lives. The newspaper, made up by our kids, shows Diane and I at twenty-one years of age. It also has individual photos of our children as young adults — Jim the oldest followed by Marcella, and the twins Leanna and Melissa. It is amazing to look at those photos then glance over the wall to see a variety of photos of their own children.

Not all the photos bring back happy memories. There is the one of Diane, her brother, sister, mom, and dad standing on the deck with the lake as a backdrop. On her mother's cheek is a dark patch, the centre of radiation therapy for the mouth cancer that later took her life.

There are no photos of my parents, both of whom died young and did not get to see Shaman's Rock, but would have loved it.

Farther along the wall is a photo of my aunt Terri Hungle and her husband Gus. Uncle Gus wired Shaman's Rock cottage twenty-seven years ago. He designated me his apprentice, drilling holes, stringing wire, making connections, and taught me how not to electrocute myself. Although he owned a large electrical contracting business that wired many of the industrial sites in Sarnia, Gus was nervous about the final cottage electrical inspection. The inspector had a reputation for disliking out-of-area electricians. Gus was quiet and respectful as the inspector went through the cottage. At the end of his tour the inspector complained that receptacle distances were not correct and would have to be redone. Gus lost his patience. He exploded, citing by heart the electrical code section relating to receptacle distances. The inspector stared at him, signed the final inspection report, and left without a word.

There are, of course, many pictures of people holding fish. Closer examination of the photos leaves me disturbed. There are photos of Jessica, from child to young woman holding fish, all of which appear to be more than four pounds. Even her mother, my daughter-in-law Patricia, is holding a whopper that I recall was five-pounds plus.

There is grandson John with a nice fish, and his brother Marcus and also eldest grandson Robert, who does not profess to be an angler. Then there is me, holding a 1.5-inch sunfish. My eyes rescan the wall desperately. Surely there must be a photo of me holding a trophy. There is not, and the truth slaps me in the face; all those smiling faces are beaming with angling success. Every one, except mine.

Well, photos never tell the whole story, so I move along. There is a photo of Peanuts, our little dog who was terrified of the forest. She hated when we walked the snowmobile track into Shaman's Rock in the darkness after a long week of work in the city. A wolf would howl and she would take off like a frightened deer. We would catch up to her later, pressed hard against the cottage door, eyes bugged out like Ichabod Crane after he had been chased through Sleepy Hollow by the Headless Horseman.

There are numerous campfire pictures, of course. Even a couple of trophy presentations taken at the annual Shaman's Rock Invitational Golf Tournament, an exclusive two-and-one-half-day event celebrating bad golf and good friendship. Only four people have ever been invited, me and three close friends. We are all winners because of that friendship.

There are special moments on the wall. Jim, his son Robert, and me posing with the cedar strip canoe Jim restored and gave to Diane and me for a special anniversary. The photo reminds me of my grandfather, Robert Lee Poling, who paddled his twelve-foot canoe, The Undertaker, thirty kilometres from the Port Arthur waterfront out to the Sleeping Giant. To the surprise of everyone who knew him, he died of natural causes and never did drown as had been predicted.

Most of the pictures are of kids, and they are a reminder that kids should not be stuck in the city, knowing nothing but concrete and asphalt. It is important for them to experience the natural world.

The wall is filled now, but I have a stack of new photos ready to go up. One of these days I'll have to start thinking about a second picture wall.

— 12 —
CAMPFIRES

"Fire is the best of servants; but what a master!"
— THOMAS CARLYLE, *PAST AND PRESENT*

We are all gathered around the campfire overlooking our lake when I see it. I lean forward in my chair and squint. There it is. Definitely a light on the rocky point across the water.

There is an abandoned cottage, dilapidated and mysterious, on the point, so it is odd to see a light there. It has been many years since anyone connected to that property has been there. I have seen the light before but it takes me several viewings to figure it out. It is mid-June and the sun is late setting. This isn't exactly the Far North, but the sun sets just after nine o'clock and we have to start our evening campfire before dark, otherwise the little kids will be up too late.

The light is not a mysterious prowler, nor a ghost on the tumble-down place on the point. It is that final ray of the sun, setting in west, bouncing off the water and onto what's left of the glass windows on the cabin.

No use ruining a good story with the facts, however. So, I alert the kids to the light across the lake and begin telling them about the light at The Cabin at Ghostly Point. It's about a young girl, Shainie Garrison, who is sitting at the campfire and sees a mysterious light that no one else sees. She is determined to discover the light's source. The next morning she paddles her canoe to the point, where she begins a dangerous adventure that ends with more mystery.

The kids are mesmerized by the story, made spookier by the darkness closing in on our little patch of campfire space. It gets told every year at the campfire, a genuine cottage tradition.

The cabin is gone now, razed by government people who considered it a hazard, which it probably was. The story remains. It can be found in my e-book *Lights in Dark Forests*, available at *Amazon.ca*, *Smashwords.com*, or other places where electronic books live.

The mournful call of a single loon is the cue for another story: the Story of the Loon. It is a fantasy in which an elder in a native village creates a new bird that will warn about dangers to the environment. He is laughed into banishment but spends his life raising the birds on northern lakes. The kids love it, and when they hear a loon, they think of the environment.

The cottage campfire is a magical thing, especially in a society driven half-mad by cell phones, texting, Facebook, Twitter, and all the other quick hits of less-than-thoughtful communication.

Slip out of the darkness and take a seat on the log where a dozen people are gathered, staring pensively into the flames dancing inside the circle of granite stones. The first thing you will notice is the silence. People are in no hurry to talk. When someone does speak, it is not in the short, sharp pings so common in today's wired society. It is often slow, measured, and even thoughtful.

A campfire's magic slows people's heartbeats, thought processes, and their tongues. The flames are speed bumps along the path between grey matter and lips. It is hard to imagine hearing around the campfire the tactless snippets of comment that zip daily across omnipresent blogs. The campfire draws people into itself and absorbs the heat from over-spinning minds, redistributing it as reflection, focus, and warm good feelings.

As complicated as the world has become, the campfire has remained the same over the millenniums since fire was discovered. It is the same at St. Nora Lake as the campfires that flicker along the coast of the Great Australian Bight, the Congo jungle, or somewhere in the mountains of Afghanistan.

Of all the animals on earth, humans are the only ones who have a primal instinct to gather beside fire, which offers warmth, protection, and light in a world of darkness. Humans are the only animals that have come to understand and use fire. All other animals fear it, another reason why humans find security within the campfire circle. It has been at least 500,000 years since the first campfires appeared, yet our fascination with them has not dimmed.

Over those thousands of years we have solved all the mysteries of fires, except one. We know everything about fire from how humans acquired it (lightning) to the number of BTUs each fire log of different woods will produce. What we don't know is why kids must poke at a campfire with sticks. Well, not just kids; there is an irrepressible urge in most of us to poke at a fire. As the American writer Charles Dudley Warner wrote more than 100 years ago: "To poke a wood fire is more solid enjoyment than almost anything else in the world."

Kids take it farther by swirling the fiery poker stick in the air like a sparkler, an act which usually brings raised adult growls of, "Leave that stick in the fire or I'll take it away from you!"

The waving of fiery sticks is perhaps preferable to that other campfire threat; the gooey marshmallow. When a kid drops one into your hands, you're done for the night. You have no more chance shedding the stickiness than Lady Macbeth had of rubbing out that damn spot.

No one knows for sure who was the first to bring the marshmallow menace to the campfire. We know the Egyptians created a sticky confection 2,000 years ago by making honey candy and thickening it with the sap of the marsh mallow plant. Late in the 1800s someone invented a way of using corn starch to make marshmallow moulds.

How people started toasting marshmallows over a fire is not known. We do know that the Girl Scout Handbook published in 1927 gave the recipe for toasting a marshmallow over a campfire and squashing it between two Graham crackers. This sticky treat became known as the s'more, presumably a contraction of "some more." There now is a National S'Mores Day, celebrated on August 10.

I celebrate the s'more every time I try to rise from my campfire chair and discover some kid has left a piece of s'more or toasted marshmallow on the seat. No matter what their claims, there is no laundry detergent that will take roasted marshmallow out of the seat of a pair of jeans in one try.

Campfires come in all forms and sizes. Some folks like big fires, with singing and skits. Others like the simple, reflective campfires in which much thinking and little talking is done. And there are the serious campfires — council fires in which the business of the gathering is discussed. I like the reflective type, when long periods of silence are broken by someone raising a profound thought or launching a ghost story.

Ours is a fragmented world. People have so many different interests and opinions, and so many opportunities to pursue them. There now are more things that draw people apart than there are things that draw them together. The campfire draws us together into that circle of glow in the dark forests. At the campfire, we are much the same: vulnerable creatures who face many risks when we step alone into the dark beyond the campfire. Within the circle we are not alone.

Flames dancing inside a campfire circle are spiritual. They encourage attitudes that create fellowship, goodwill, decency, love. They deliver to us calm in a world of uncalm.

John James Audubon, American woodsman who studied and drew birds and for whom the National Audubon Society is named, once described how he felt about a campfire: "no one can have an idea of what a good fire is who has never seen a campfire in the woods of America."

— 13 —
FISHING

"You know why there are so many whitefish in the
Yellowstone River? Because the Fish and Game people have
never done anything to help them."
— RUSSELL CHATHAM, *SILENT SEASONS*

I look up from the dock to see Diane waving goodbye. She is hanging out clothes. I smile and give my six-horse Evinrude a gentle pat on the engine cover before I head out onto the lake. I am not smiling because I am going fishing while she does housework. I am smiling at the contradictions between her work machines and my little Evinrude. Several washers, fridges, and stoves have come and gone from the cottage while the Evinrude has been around for half a century.

I attach its tank, pump the line ball twice, pull the choke and yank the pull cord twice. It fires up, belching thick white smoke from the fuel conditioner I added last November when I put it away.

I know the old Evinrude is not environmentally friendly. The new four-stroke engines are much cleaner and I nurse some guilt that I have not made the change. There is, however, a limit to how much I can spend to help save the environment. Changing both my two-cycle motors would cost at least $10,000.

Then there is the issue of dependability. What else works so well after fifty years of use, spending every winter in an unheated shed? If everything today was built as well as these old motors, we'd never have to replace anything. Then I suppose the economy would collapse.

What would collapse, if left solely to me, would be the fishing tackle industry. I seldom buy any new tackle, despite being a master of neglect when it comes to my fishing stuff. That is a terrible admission, but it is true.

Just to get out on the lake it has taken me a day of untangling, sorting, and cleaning the fishing gear stored unused for months in the musty gloom of the waterfront shed where fishing and boating stuff is kept.

I've had to push my way through mounds of life jackets, deck chairs, paddles, and a bucket of treasured plumbing junk to get rods and reels, nets, and minnow buckets — the gear of the summer cottage fisher. All this stuff lounges in corners, rests crookedly against walls, or hangs from fat building spikes driven into rough studs.

Fishing gear is the most taken-for-granted of all cottage stuff. It's hauled out in early summer, dragged through sun, sand, and water, then unceremoniously plunked into the tool shed in fall. This stuff needs some tender care but regrettably does not get it at my cottage, nor at most others.

However, once a year I swallow hard and plunge into the mess. Reels need cleaning, lubricating, and fixing. The tip of my favourite little graphite rod (the one I call Black Death) is missing, likely caught in a slammed door. The old Berkley Cherrywood bought for $9.99 decades ago is showing its age with line grooves in its metal guides.

The grandkids' rods still hold spinners and hooks with the mummified remains of worms last dunked seven months ago. Then there are the reels, some choked with backlash, some with rotting line, others with no line at all. Reels that sound like pepper grinders when their cranks are turned.

After a couple of hours I have set up the reels and dabbed them lightly with oil, and replaced the six or eight strands of cotton backing that cushions the new monofilament line I have installed. I have been careful not to overfill the reels. Spinning reels should be filled to one-eighth of an inch from the top of the spool. If you overfill a reel you will have the line constantly falling off the spool and tangling. If you underfill it, you don't get good casting length.

I check the rods for cracks in the line guides and for unravelling of the thread that holds the guides. Thread is easily kept in place by applying some nail polish or varnish. I also rub the joints of break-down rods with candle wax to allow the pieces to slip together easier.

The oldest rod, a 1950s first-of-its-kind fibreglass fly rod, now has been retired and hangs in an honoured place inside the cottage. It was my dad's and I remember him — tall and lean in a fedora and granny glasses — working that rod over a stream like it was a magic wand. Whenever I read the novella *A River Runs Through It* I picture my dad on the banks of Little Bear Creek outside Schreiber, Ontario, that rod moving the flies just above the dancing waters of the creek.

The tackle boxes just need some sorting and cleaning and I am ready to float out and away from cottage chores.

St. Nora is typical of the 2,200 lake trout lakes in Ontario. It is nestled in pre-Cambrian bedrock with water that is forty metres deep in spots, well oxygenated and cold, although not nearly as cold as it used to be. Our trout are descendants of the original Haliburton wild trout strain, a throwback to the end of the ice age. These trout are known for their rapid growth, torpedo-shaped bodies, and vigorous fighting abilities.

In 1987 the Ontario government raised an alarm about lake trout populations being in trouble. That was no big surprise. The folks who fish the trout saw it long before and saw it worsen very quickly. In 1987–88 I was still catching my one or two spring dinner trout by trolling St. Nora's shoreline for one to two hours. Today, you can fish for two hours without getting a bite, and last year there was no spring trout dinner.

The Environmental Commissioner of Ontario has warned, "The weight of existing evidence indicates there is cause for serious concern about the sustainability of the lake trout and the fishery, particularly in the southern part of the province." It told the Ministry of Natural Resources to get off its butt and devote more money and staff to fixing the problem.

The ugly truth is that there is no fix. Lake trout now fight for food with rock bass, non-native pike, and other unwanted species brought in as bait minnows by gormless anglers. They have been overfished in winter because anglers on snow machines have easy access to lakes never winter fished before.

The snowmobile, which provides much enjoyable outdoor recreation to many, has done much to diminish trout fishing. My grandfather, who guided outside Sault Ste. Marie in the Dirty Thirties, once told me about a productive lake north of the Sault, which few people ever visited. It was a dream fishing spot reached by portaging a canoe. In the 1960s when the first snowmobiles appeared, I borrowed one and drove into the lake and found it dotted with ice fishermen taking full counts, and more, of big speckled trout. A few years of winter fishing killed it.

Invasive species, shoreline development, acid rain, and other man-created habitat threats are killing the trout fisheries. You won't be putting a fork in too many more lake trout. It's pretty much all over, folks, especially in the southern part of the lake trout range.

I always think back on a suggestion raised many years ago by John M. Casselman, a well respected and long-time Ontario government biologist. Casselman theorized that mature female lake trout have more energy demands during the summer because their gonads are developing for the fall spawning season. He figured the percentage of female angling catches rose to as high as 70 percent during the summer, while females represented only 13 percent of the overall lake trout population.

The math shows that summer fishing can be devastating to female lake trout just as they are getting ready to produce new generations. I often wonder why Casselman's work did not develop into summer fishing restrictions.

A lack of fish never has been a reason for me not to go fishing. Anyone who fishes with me always catches more than I do. No matter, fishing is about atmosphere and ambience and being at peace with your surroundings. When the water is flat and still like a mirror you get double pleasure from the shoreline. The jumbled beauty of trees and rocks shows itself a second time as it projects itself onto the glassy water.

The bow of the little boat shatters the reflections, but they quickly piece themselves back together, no worse for wear. The motor does little to disturb the peace; it is small and old and purrs quietly out of respect for the soothing tranquility this lake gives.

Trolling for lake trout is when I do my best thinking. I think about things I am writing, or will write. I compose stuff in my head, and when my memory starts overloading I just think about life. Often I will drink a bottle of beer and smoke a cigar while trolling. I know that having a beer in the boat is illegal, and smoking a cigar, even though I don't inhale, is unhealthy and not socially correct. I guess it's just my small way of rebelling against a society that seems to spend more of its time telling me who I should be and how I should act.

Today the wind is up from the northwest, pushing little whitecaps against the boat. The wind quickens into little gusts that force the lake to spit in my face, perhaps as a warning that it is time to head back. It is hard to hold a trolling rod and manage the boat.

Being out here is becoming uncomfortable and I wonder if they teach you how to handle this kind of weather in those laughable government-mandated courses and exams that you must take to operate a boat.

Diane had to pay sixty bucks for one of those courses to get a boating licence. I don't have a licence but I did take a Power Squadron course one winter in Vancouver decades ago and recall its exam being not too much less difficult than the one they give you to qualify for a pilot's licence. Which sets me thinking about how lucky I am to be out here fighting waves of water instead of being in the city fighting new and higher waves of government.

Big government is always with us, however. Even out here on the lake. To get out here today I needed to follow the rules and pay the taxes of a variety of government bureaucracies. If my engine was slightly bigger I would need a federal boat registration. I also have to have government-approved life jackets, government-mandated bailing kit with flashlight and throw rope, and government-approved gas containers.

For autumn fishing I sometimes carry a small shotgun in case I want to stop, stretch my legs in the forest, and look for upland game. On those days I need to have a licence to possess the gun, proof of gun registration, a provincial hunting licence for upland birds, a federal licence for water-fowl, boating licence, and provincial fishing licence.

My mind thankfully is diverted from the horrors of bureaucracy by a snag. I break my line and haul out my tackle bag where I keep monofilament tippet leader in a side pocket reserved for my fly fishing reels. I have neglected to check this pocket in my frenzy of tackle organization and cleaning. I reach in and remove remains of two reel bags. They have been shredded into balls of nest material filled with mice turds. Mice have wintered here, chewing anything soft to make a more comfortable nest. They have not bothered the reels but they have chewed into nothingness my package of monofilament leader.

Fishing is over for today. Too much wind, chewed leaders, and no fish. That's all right, because it's not about the fishing. Just being out here was enough.

— 14 —
TURNOVER

"Nature hates calculators."
— Ralph Waldo Emerson

A strange thing happens to the lake in summer. It turns itself over, sort of like flipping an omelette — the warm side goes to the top, the cool side to the bottom. It's called stratification, in which the warm upper water is separated from the cold stuff by a dividing line called the thermocline.

In cottage language, the summer sun warms the top of the lake. Warm water is less dense than cold water and sits on top of the cold. Warm and cold layers do not mix much, especially in stable summer weather. When this happens, the lake trout head below the thermocline into their preferred colder water. Above the thermocline, the warmer-water fish such as bass and panfish are active.

St. Nora's lake trout might be diminishing, but the bass and pike are doing well. The lake has smallmouth bass, which don't like water that is below fifteen degrees or above twenty-seven Celsius.

Smallmouth are golden bronze and green fish with dark vertical bronze markings along their sides, and a spiny dorsal fin that will prick your fingers if you are not careful when handling them. They average one to two pounds, but we've seen them up to six pounds at St. Nora. The Ontario record is 9.84 pounds.

The guy on our lake who really knows bass and how to catch them is Mike Jones, a master bass fisherman who lives in Maryland when he's not at St. Nora. Mike has one of those sleek and shiny bass boats with an outboard motor that has forty times more power than my little six-horse Evinrude.

When it screams down the lake, Mike's bass boat looks like a large pencil propelled by rocket fuel. It goes so fast that it seems like the hull might set the water on fire. The force of the wind it creates pushes your life jacket up against your throat and leaves you struggling for breath. It will do over 110 kilometres an hour across calm water.

The whole idea of the bass boat is to get from one spot to another very quickly. These things are designed for tournament fishing. If the big guys are not biting in one spot, you race to the next to get your line in before another competitor.

The bass boat is basically a cockpit for two or three people, with flat front and rear decks on which to stand and cast lures. They have fish-holding tanks, electric motors for moving the boat around slowly and quietly during fishing, and various electronic gear for studying the water and finding fish. New ones can cost in the $40,000 to $50,000 range.

Tournament fishing for major money is a mania in the United States and has caught on in Canada in recent years.

Mike guides bass fishermen on Lake Anna outside Washington, D.C., and also makes and sells Pappy's Baits in the U.S., plastic offerings for bass, in a never-ending quest to find the ultimate bait that will catch the big ones under any condition. Up here he fishes just for personal pleasure and practice. His bass boat has been a feature on our lake for many years, coming and going from St. Margaret Island, where he and his wife Dianne have been popular summer residents for many years.

The opening of bass season usually corresponds with the arrival of cottage summer guests. One morning you wake up and a troop of little kids, all wearing life jackets and holding fishing rods, is standing by your bedside. All kids love fishing. Some tire of it more quickly than others, but they all start off fascinated by it. Some are natural anglers. Our first grandchild, Jessica, took to it instantly and, now a university graduate, still likes to get out on a lake or stream.

A younger grandchild, John, is one of those people with a knack for catching fish. He catches them when no one else is getting a bite. There are people like that, coated with some type of magic attraction jelly.

Jessica's younger brother, Robert, never took to it. He did go out on the lake one time recently with his dad, however. They had been fishing for a short time when Robert became serious and said, "Dad, I need to tell you something."

His dad braced himself and replied in his bravest voice:

"Go ahead. You know we can talk about anything." Anything likely was going to be bad. He wanted to drop out of university, had got caught speeding, or even something worse.

Robert fiddled with his fishing rod, then stared at his dad.

"I just don't get it."

"You don't get what?" Jim asked.

"This. This being out in the boat waiting for a fish. I just don't get it."

Patience and organization will not guarantee the sanity of a mentor of child anglers, but they certainly help. He or she must go out on the lake being prepared to deal calmly with rats' nest backlashes, hooks waving dangerously everywhere, battles over the best fishing positions in the boat and cries of "It stole my worm."

The main thing to remember is that kids are out there to catch fish. So it's a mistake to take them out in pursuit of lunker bass or trout. That might work for people who really know how to catch fish, but it doesn't work for me. I take the little guys down to the back bay at the east end

Photograph by Marcella Austenfeld.

Most kids are enthralled by fishing, but they can become bored very quickly. To keep them interested we take them to a shallow back bay where there are hundreds of hungry little perch, pumpkinseed, and rock bass.

of the lake. It is shallow and weedy there and out of the most annoying breezes that continually move the boat while you are trying to keep kids in their places. It also is filled with hungry little pumpkinseeds, perch, and rock bass. Also, it's an easy spot to rescue any rambunctious child who falls overboard.

The best days in the little bay are filled with shouts of "I've got one!" and "I need another worm." And "Aww, it's too early to go back."

You hear lots of that every July at the Dorset Kids Fish Derby, part of Ontario's family fishing day. Kids twelve and under line the public dock at the Trading Bay narrows for two hours of catch and release fishing. Every kid gets a prize, even if he or she doesn't catch a fish, so everyone goes home happy.

These are some of the cottage moments that will live in the minds of these kids until they are old like me.

— 15 —
SOLOING

"Adventure is worthwhile in itself."
— AMELIA EARHART

The sounds of summer are not always happy sounds.

"Dad, Jim's been bitten by a snake," is one unhappy sound I remember well. The two youngest girls, the twins, brought the news breathlessly from a swampy area where a creek flows out of the lake.

Jim, the oldest, appeared soon after, head hung low and left hand clutching his right arm. He had a half-moon of tiny teeth marks in the fleshy area between his thumb and pointer finger. We cleaned the bite but when he complained that pain was progressing up his arm and into his neck, we took him to hospital.

The only poisonous snakes in Ontario are the near-extinct Massasauga Rattlesnake, and bites from these, like any pit viper, leave two distinct fang punctures. The doctors were intrigued and guessed that a non-venomous snake had hit a nerve that was radiating pain up the arm. Crisis over.

We all learned important life lessons from the snake bite incident: there are risks in letting kids explore nature, but they must explore nature, and all of us must do our best to manage the risks. Certainly Jim learned that you don't irritate God's little creatures by grabbing them by the tails.

We also learned that at a cottage you need to think about accidents and illness before they happen. Where do you take someone who has broken an arm or is suffering a heart attack? Which hospital is closest? What types of care does it provide? If time is not critical would it be better to get home to your own hospital, doctors, and medical records? We all tend to think about these things when an emergency occurs. We need to run them through our heads before something happens.

Accidents happen at cottages, usually when people are least expecting them. When we were building the interior of Shaman's Rock, Jim was the centre of another incident in which we were mere millimetres away from losing our only son.

We had erected scaffolding and groups of friends and relatives were nailing pine boards onto the high ceiling. The scaffolding boards were heavy, undressed timbers, just under three metres long. The guys at the very top were moving two of the timbers when one slipped and fell headlong straight down.

Jim was directly under the scaffolding preparing a pine board. I happened to look up, saw the timber slip, and yelled to him. He had only time move his head. The timber missed his head by centimetres, grazed his shoulder and back, and almost broke through the floor. Jim was scraped and bruised but nothing was broken.

Incidents like that make you wonder if you can ever be too safe when it comes to kids. Yet, in trying to keep cottage kids safe, we often deprive them of the joys and rich experiences of cottage life.

Today's children live childhoods without the benefits of many nature experiences. Television, computers, electronic games — all occupy times once spent kicking cans through fields, building play forts in the woods, climbing trees, and exploring creek beds. Life for so many kids now days is bubble wrapped, connected to life lessons by USB ports.

"We've socialized movement out of the lives of our kids for the convenience of parents and institutions," Mark Tremblay, the chief scientific officer of Active Healthy Kids Canada was quoted in the *Globe and Mail* newspaper. "From a very young age all they hear is: 'Sit still,' 'no running,' 'do your homework, don't go outside,' 'wait for a ride,' and so on," Dr. Tremblay said. "When you impose a structure of inactivity you see the results we're seeing."

It's not their fault. The child's world is filled with the dangers of human predators, traffic, shrinking natural areas, and many distractions. We are starting to see the impacts of this as childhood obesity from lack of exercise, stress, and a lack of understanding of the natural world in which we are all players. The Canadian Obesity Foundation reports that in 2011, 26 percent of kids ages two to seventeen were overweight, triple the number of twenty-five years earlier.

One expert, child advocate Richard Louv, even links "denatured childhood" to attention-deficit hyperactivity disorder. His assessment of the growing problem, and more importantly some thoughts on how to attack it, are written in his book *Last Child in the Woods: Saving Our Children from Nature-deficit Disorder* (Algonquin Books, 2005). Louv's book started an international movement to get children back outside and involved with nature.

I get to see nature-deficit children at our cottage. If you let them, they will gravitate inside to the TV and the handheld game boxes. When they do, they miss another opportunity to see, hear, and feel the natural world and understand that we are part of the wildness of it.

We had a teenage kid visit Shaman's Rock one weekend and he seemed to enjoy the outside activities. He went swimming in the lake, then ran into the cottage and went directly to the bathroom where we heard the shower running. When he emerged, someone asked him what he was doing. He explained that he had taken a shower. Why after an hour of swimming in the lake would he take a shower? The water was dark-looking, he said, so it probably was full of "stuff." I didn't have the heart to tell him that our cottage uses water pumped directly from the lake.

At the cottage, the easiest way of keeping kids safe is not to let them do anything that might involve the slightest danger. When we do that we deprive them of important learning experiences, and ourselves of the joy of witnessing the world opening up to them.

Yes, there are dangers, but restricting kids' access to nature is not the answer. If they don't go outside at the cottage, how are they going to learn about smelts, dandelions, maple syrup, canoes, and even outboard motors?

Kids learn from doing things, often in their own way. One day I decided it was time for a grandson to learn how to run the little twelve-foot boat with the six-horsepower motor. I went over all the safety issues with him, including checking the amount of gasoline in the portable gas tank.

"Lift it up and you can tell how much is in it by the weight," I said, explaining that the mechanical gas gauges in these things are not always accurate.

He strained to lift the tank. "Yep, it's heavy," he said.

We were fishing the farthest reach of the lake when the motor died. I tried restarting it without success. I checked the gas line, then lifted the tank. It fairly flew into the air from its lightness. Totally empty.

"I thought you checked the tank," I said.

"I did," said the grandson. "It was heavy."

An hour and a half later, my arms and back aching from rowing, we reached our dock. Then it struck me: even an empty tank feels heavy to an eight-year-old.

— 16 —
PORTAGES

Young Billy Ray: "A canoe! Just like the Indians used."
Old Norman: "Actually, the Indians used a different grade
of aluminum."
— FROM THE MOVIE *ON GOLDEN POND*

They slip silently through the early morning mist cuddling the far shore. Four canoes carrying two people each and heading northeast toward the back bay and the uphill portage into Sherborne Lake. They have launched their canoes at the Frost Centre on the western shore of the lake, and it takes less than half an hour across mainly protected waters to reach the portage at the bottom of the creek that connects Sherborne Lake with St. Nora. Then the work begins. It is 813 metres, some of it slightly uphill, to Sherborne Lake Dam. Once they reach Sherborne, the water trails and portages will take them almost anywhere in Haliburton County, even up to Algonquin Park and beyond.

I often sit on Shaman's Rock and watch the canoe trippers pass, wondering how many trippers, voyageurs, explorers, and Indian parties have passed here over the decades. What adventures they must have had! What stories they would have had to tell! Imagine if we were able to go back in time and listen to their campfire conversations.

I've trekked the mud and rock Sherborne portage many times myself, branching off sometimes to Big Hawk and Nunikani, or up the hill and along the bug-infested trail to Silver Doe and Silver Buck, two lovely little lakes tied together by an outfall that spills over the rocks between the two.

There were always makeshift campsites along these trails but now governments have become involved. The Township of Algonquin

Highlands has started managing water and portage travel over the vast wilderness known as the Frost Centre lands. These lands stretch from St. Nora up to the edges of Algonquin Park, covering sixty lakes, seventy portages, and 171 campsites.

Camping is allowed only on official campsites. Four campers were fined $950 last year for camping on a site other than one authorized by the government. Sites cost $12 per person per night. So two canoes of two people each, out for five nights on the trail, will pay $240 for their camping privileges. It seems like a lot to me, but I'm of the generation that was used to not paying anything on lands owned by the taxpayers. The fees are part of life now: governments will create revenue streams wherever they can.

There are five campsites on our lake, one directly across from Shaman's Rock. It is on a rocky isthmus that sticks out from the granite and pine cliffs and gets the evening sun. There used to be a cabin there, the cabin I called the Cabin at Ghostly Point in my campfire story told to the kids.

Watercolour by Jim Poling, the author's son.

The old cabin is gone now, but Ghostly Point, and the story it inspired, remain a part of life at Shaman's Rock. "The Cabin at Ghostly Point" is a story told around the campfire every summer.

It was a squatter's cottage for decades. There is no written history to the place, but the story is that it was one of a couple hunting cabins built on the lake during the late 1920s or 1930s. It became a family summer cabin, but the folks who owned it grew old and passed, apparently leaving it to a new generation who were not interested.

There were hundreds, perhaps thousands of similar cabins built on Crown land throughout Ontario. Sometimes people who held them applied to government to buy the land and get an official deed. The Killabys, who started on St. Nora with a similar hunt camp did that and now have a spectacular cottage at the east end of the lake where the old hunt camp used to be.

The people who squatted on Ghostly Point apparently never applied for a deed. The story goes that the government was trying to clean up some of these squatting situations and asked the inheritors of the point if they were interested in getting legal ownership. The answer, apparently, was no and the government decided to fold the parcel back into the Crown lands surrounding it.

The cabin on the point was unique. It had a porch for sitting out and taking the evening sun. It was starting to fall apart, and in fact was a danger to kids who boated to the point and would explore inside. Some of the floorboards were rotting, windows had been smashed.

One March, perhaps six or eight years ago, we saw a couple of men on the snowy point, and smoke rising. Then we saw flames licking the sky above the treetops. The government had sent in a crew to burn the place. In the spring, another crew came in and cleaned up some of the charred remains and broken glass. Then the official campsite sign went up.

My dad used to tell me about the government burning fish and hunt cabins in northwestern Ontario. The northern bush had many such shacks, used by men hunting and fishing for food during the Depression. My dad said the government sent crews in to burn many of these, including one built by my grandfather and his pals.

Fees for enjoying our outdoor heritage have become an annoyance to many. On a recent fishing trip to northwestern Ontario we paid roughly $35 for a one-night campsite at Lake Superior Provincial Park west of Sault Ste. Marie. The fee is close to $40 if you want electricity. For our fee we got a patch of beaten down ground with a fire pit, some dirty out-houses, and a shower building that was sort of okay.

On the return trip we stopped at Katherine Cove in the same park where the Ontario government charges $4 for each car that stops for a washroom break or to have a sandwich. Payment was by automated credit card machine.

What irritates is not so much the fee, but the fee versus the value. When a fee does not match value, it is simply just another tax, a blatant government move to take money because it is entitled to it. And, of course, the cavalier fashion in which governments spend what they collect from us also grates.

The average cottager thinks hard before spending. Many cottage projects go on hold until the needed money is at least in sight. Govern-ments tend to spend whether they have the money or not, thus today's whopping deficits.

At any rate, nothing is free nowadays. Whatever the fees, campers, canoe trippers, and other outdoor enthusiasts have to accept them. The same as cottagers have to accept rising taxes, insurance, and elec-trical costs.

Cottage prices and costs have risen so much you wonder if anyone can afford them. However, Ellen Wiley, friend and realtor in Dorset, tells me that it is easier to afford a cottage now than fifteen or twenty years ago. Financing generally is easier. Interest rates are much lower. There still are many cottages in the $250,000 range. Also, more people are retiring and downsizing, which provides money for luxuries like a cottage.

Large, very expensive places continue to sell as well, says Ellen. That's because some find a cottage a better investment than what they see in the stock markets.

She says cottaging has changed dramatically in the last twenty years. That's because work habits have changed. People need to be connected at the cottage — through land phones, cell networks, the Internet. Cot-tages more and more are becoming homes away from home.

Ellen saw a transition begin in the late 1980s and continue until now when many cottages are summer homes.

Brad Robinson, lifetime Dorset resident who owns the hardware and supermarket, notes a huge increase in the number of winter cottages. Snowmobiles, the four-wheel drive SUV, improved winter access, and cottages more built like homes.

The changes will continue. Don't be surprised if one day you beach your canoe at a deep forest campsite and see a sign: WI-FI HOTSPOT.

— 17 —
THE BUNK HOUSE

"The poorest man may in his cottage bid defiance to all the
forces of the Crown."
— WILLIAM PITT, THE ELDER

I t sits alone on a terraced area just above the lakeshore, and ten metres
down the hill from our cottage. It's empty of human presence, except
when summer visitors come, and the little building has much time to
reflect on how our cottage life has changed with passing times.

The bunkhouse is a cool hideaway with humble beginnings. It started
life at St. Nora Lake as an outhouse, then graduated to a storage shed
when running water arrived at the main building. It was our only refuge
when we first discovered the lake. It held all our tools when we arrived for
weekends of lot clearing and building. When it rained we could huddle in
there among the chainsaw, grub hoes, shovels, and various other pieces
of hand equipment.

I remember falling against it and breaking my shoulder when we
decided to tear much of it apart and rebuild it. We used parts of the
original structure, and with piles of store-bought materials and some
scavenged siding, soon had a twelve- by eight-foot building with a little
storage loft and hinged windows.

The place was sort of a bunkhouse, a place where people could sleep
in an emergency, but mainly it was a storage place. It reflected the activity
of our cottage lives. Stored there was the ice auger and minnow bucket
for winter fishing. There were water skis and various water toys.

Now the bunkhouse reflects a different stage. It is an acceptable living
quarters needed by a family tripled in size by in-laws and grandchildren.

No cottage tools or toys are stored there anymore. They have been replaced by a small television set, a must for grandchildren who now are the main occupants. There are bookshelves filled with interesting things to read, including my collection of Ernest Gann, the pilot, sailor, author, and screenwriter who wrote flying classics such as *The High and Mighty*, *Island in the Sky*, and *The Aviator*.

Visitors to our bunkhouse often remark how warm, comfortable, cozy, and quiet it is. "So this is where you do all your writing!"

I hate to disappoint them, but it is not where I write. It is difficult to write there because I hear little noises that set me to worrying that the squirrels and mice are back and trying to regain control of the place. I know they are not because there is no evidence of them, but still I worry and it breaks my concentration.

I seldom write anywhere at the cottage. There are too many distractions: loons calling on the lake, raucous crows going back and forth in the trees, firewood that needs splitting, nails that need hammering, and people to enjoy. And too many ways to goof off.

The bunkhouse might not see much writing activity, but it does get to see a lot of thinking and reflection, and of course hears the whispers and laughter of the children. Cottage bunkhouses are special places for children. They are the favoured destination for kids who slip the grip of adult supervision. A place to go to share secrets and to enjoy some independence.

There is a voice inside all of us, whispering seductively, telling us to find a secluded spot and to build a hideaway. I often think of building a log hideaway up our back hill. A log retreat with a woodstove and a porch overlooking the lake. I need another building like I need galloping hiccups. It is ridiculous to think about building another retreat, no matter how small, but the urge is there. Our son also wants to build a little log hideaway on the height of land in the bush behind the cottage.

We have absolutely everything we need already at Shaman's Rock. However, the riches that we have in a wonderful cottage, spectacular view, and plenty of property do not smother the primeval instinct to build shelter. Get something over your head, build a fire, cook meat.

Until recently, our bunkhouse was not on our property. It sat on a shoreline road allowance, those arcane scraps of land held by governments. These allowances date back to settlement days. Most of them were twenty metre strips of land around a lake or along a river. They were put there to allow public passage to and from those waterways. For instance, someone in a storm could land on the shore for safety without fear of being thrown off for trespassing.

Development of roads into and along lakes made these allowances useless in most cases. In recent times in Ontario, the provincial government decided that all these bits and pieces of shoreline land were useless to anyone but a cottager, and began allowing local municipalities to sell them off.

We knew we had the twenty metre shoreline allowance in front of our cottage. We also knew that a couple lots down from us the allowance ran into the lake. No road could be built there, so we didn't worry about it. To buy the allowance would mean a significant layout of money and more annual property tax.

Still, there was the lingering worry that anyone could land on our shore and camp out. The land belonged to government, therefore presumably the people. Also, there were building restrictions on the allowances; you couldn't build a boathouse, or a bunkhouse for that matter. We built the bunkhouse and hoped no township official would ever pass by and take note of it. After almost twenty-five years we had a chance to acquire the road allowance at a reasonable price, so we took it.

Many cottage properties have a road allowance of some sort, and cottagers, and potential cottagers, should be aware of them and the problems they might pose. Cottage buyers should ask a lot of questions to ensure they get a full understanding of allowances, what they mean, and how they might restrict you.

There are some key types of road allowances to keep in mind: a regular township road through private land but maintained by the township, a township road allowance that is not maintained by the township, or a road through Crown land built by cottagers and maintained by cottagers. Also there are road allowances that provide right of way across cottage properties so other cottagers can get to their properties. And road allowances that trespass on someone's property but have been used continuously for many years and pose no problem, perhaps until someone else buys the land.

Many complications can arise from these various road allowances. For instance, someone might be buying a cottage with a path that runs beside it and down to the lake. A check might reveal that it is a full road allowance and during summer it is well used by dozens and dozens of people to get to the lake for fishing, boating, swimming, or whatever. Suddenly you have a cottage with a quiet, little-used path in three seasons that becomes a nightmare of noisy activity in July and August.

David Currie, a Huntsville lawyer who handles many cottage county deals every year, gave me a brief primer on road allowances. He stressed the importance of using a real estate agent who really knows the area in which you are looking for a cottage. In the case of that path down to the lake, a sharp local real estate agent will know that while it looks quiet and little used, it is a hive of activity at the height of summer. A lawyer will know the laws, but might not have that local use knowledge.

I gather from David the thought that buying a cottage is not simply an individual effort. It needs to be a team event. First, the buyer has to gather together what he or she really wants. Then pick a local real estate agent who knows the area inside out and can apply the buyer's expectation to it. Then a good real estate lawyer tests the expectations against the laws.

In our township, Algonquin Highlands, you can build stairs, decks, docks, and pump houses and such on road allowances. You can't, however, build a bunkie or boat house without getting municipal permission. Different townships have different rules, but most likely are similar.

There is much misinformation about road allowances and their history. Anyone planning on spending time and money in cottage country would do well to get properly informed. A good place to start is at the Federation of Ontario Cottagers' Association website at *www.foca.on.ca*.

— 18 —
CIRCLE DANCING

"No sadder sound salutes you than the clear,
wild laughter of the loon."
— Celia Thaxter, *Seaward*

The first weekend of August is the big summer weekend in cottage country; the height of vacation season. Little shops, empty or even shuttered in late fall and winter, bulge with people in shorts, t-shirts, tank tops, and bathing suits. The queues are long at ice cream shops, and bakeries where holidayers are hungry for Road Kill Pie and other summer vacation treats.

Even the churches are packed late Saturday afternoon and Sunday morning. Priests, ministers, and church stewards wear huge smiles. The collection plates will overflow, and that is a good thing because these little cottage country churches need summer dollars to see them through the long, dark days of winter when most people, except for the snowmobile crowd, are reluctant to leave the cities.

I smile when I think of the collection plate passing along the aisles in one tiny cottage country church. By the time the plate reached me it always contained a fresh $100 bill. I knew who deposited that bill every Sunday — an American who spent every summer on a nearby lake, someone whose family business profited handsomely from outdoor pursuits. The weekly $100 bill was one of his ways of giving something back to cottage country.

Over in Haliburton on this August long weekend the preacher strays from a Bible theme and notes that the weather is showing signs of change. It is still hot during the day, but cooler at nights, signalling the slow slide into autumn. He is right. The long weekend in August always brings weather change. There is a tingle of crisp coolness in the evenings, prompting people to pull out sweaters and light jackets for the campfires. There is much fine weather ahead, including those spectacular golden autumn days, but the cooler nights do not let us forget that we are on the downside of summer.

This is the season of campfires. Yellow-orange lights flicker along the shoreline and across the lake at the tent campsites. People, shrouded in hoodies against the chill, are pressed close to those flames, telling stories and laughing. This is the cottage summer at its best because it is a time for forgetting past hurts, and for cementing relationships.

Social gatherings also are happening out on the lake. Or, we think they are social gatherings. Late into summer loons often gather on the lake for a mysterious activity called circle dancing. Several or more loons gather for a short, raucous ceremony that reminds me of a summer barn dance. This year we see a total of nine loons swimming in a circle in the middle of the lake. They dip their bills, stretch their necks, and sometimes stand upright while treading water. At times they make rushes across the water with their wings open and flapping.

Some biologists have said all this fuss is about mating. However, we see it every year in August when mating is long done and the chicks are born and well on their way to adulthood. Other biologists say the circle dancing has to do with territorial confrontations; other loons moving in to test the lake defences. Loons are gregarious, so I prefer to think that the loons are enjoying the last of the summer just like the folks gathered on shoreline decks during the day and the campfires at night.

There is much to talk about and to celebrate as summer closes. Many of the concerns of early spring evaporated as summer progressed. Thankfully, that often is the case.

There was worry about low water levels after the ice went out. No one could recall seeing them so low for so long. Late summer lake levels now are the highest in recent memory. All the fretting about drought connected to global warming is gone until another day.

The blue jays showed up finally, late but in good numbers. A couple of them are jumbo size, indicating that wherever they were hiding they were well fed. Grosbeaks appeared at the feeders for the first time in several years. So did the warbling vireo whose singing from dawn until dusk is enough to drive us insane. That little fellow is wonderful to have around, but sometimes he makes you thankful for hearing loss.

Bumble bees have been in abundance after some public panic about declining numbers. There are more monarch butterflies — with their tawny-orange wings and black accents — than I have seen before.

All this tells me that the worries of a new season often get exaggerated, or at least lack perspective. Yes, there is global warming. Yes, we humans are creating problems, but perspective, not panic, is needed to meet the challenges. Nature knows how to look after herself. And, despite our faults, we humans are making progress, slowly but steadily. Even the former Soviet Union states, some of the worst polluters on earth, are adapting cleaner planet policies. So is China.

Evidence in progress is seen in waste disposal practices in cottage country. Dumps there just mere years ago were a disgrace with anything just tossed anywhere. Today major recycling events are seen at cottage country waste disposal sites. Actual garbage pits have shrunk to a fraction of their previous sizes. The Lake of Bays dump just south of Dorset looks as if you can eat off the ground.

In 2013, millions of people around the world are working to protect the environment against human excesses. One hundred years earlier, only a handful of people expressed any concern as passenger pigeons, and migratory bird numbers in general, plummeted and watched some species become extinct.

A danger greater than global warming and pollution is the galloping polarization of our societies. It is excruciatingly difficult to get anything achieved these days because of polarization. Politics is stage crafting and practised for points, not for achieving a greater good. Anything the person on the opposite side of the debate offers is dismissed out of hand.

Many opinions are formed and expressed now on social networking sites, which offer little sober second thought. It's a fast society of quick hits in which more and more debate is black or white. Fading fast are the days when people studied positions, and often took pieces of several to form their own.

Today, if you don't believe every word from Al Gore or David Suzuki you are right-wing Neanderthal out to destroy the environment. If you ask pointed questions designed to penetrate information spin, and get to real facts, you are considered an enemy. Whatever happened to listening and gathering facts and compromises based on consideration of other opinions?

The world needs more cottage campfires, at which issues can be examined in softer, reflective light and without verbal heat. Thoughtless hooting, red-faced outrage, wing flapping and other forms of wild gesticulating do nothing to get answers, to help form serious opinions, or to find real solutions. We need to leave those antics to the loons out on the lake.

ANTHOCYANINS

— 19 —
ACORNS

"Autumn is a second spring where every leaf is a flower."
— ALBERT CAMUS

As usual, the change of season is announced by a new sound. I am resting in my bedroom, reading and nodding off, heavy eyes trying to focus on the page. A dull clink, followed by a clatter, chases away approaching sleep. Then another clink and clatter. Something has fallen onto the metal roof and is rolling down into the eavestrough. I pay little attention to what might have caused the noise until the middle of the night when a similar racket awakens me. There is a wind and I presume that pieces of branches are being blown onto the roof.

In the morning I step outside to investigate. There is nothing on the roof, but a check of the trough reveals a handful of brown nuts with checkered caps: acorns from the majestic red oak tree outside my window.

Interrupted sleep is one demerit point for metal roofing. I look around and see the changes that have crept up on me unnoticed. There is a wisp of wood smoke on the breeze. The sky is a chilly blue, seemingly devoid of all humidity. The trees across the lake are tinged with the first touches of colour. The dock ramp has the start of a downward slope, an indication that the lake is starting to drop to autumn levels.

The realization strikes me — autumn is upon us. I am gripped by a mini-panic at the thought of the cottage chores that must be done before the snow flies. That passes quickly, however. It is still sunny and reasonably warm, and winter seems far away, so there is time to explore the glorious fall woods and reflect on the new season.

I break open the hard brown shell of one of the acorns and remove the nut to taste. It is too bitter to eat because of its high tannin content. Red oaks like mine have a high tannin content while white oaks produce a sweeter version of the nut. You can distinguish the red oaks from the white by looking at their leaves; white oaks have rounded leaf lobes while the red have sharp pointed lobes.

Animals and birds will eat any acorns, bitter or not. There are more than sixty species of oak trees in North America and all produce edible acorns, which are little powerhouses of vegetable protein. More than one half of their bulk consists of energy-rich carbohydrates.

Which sets me thinking: if acorns are so nutritious, why is the bear from up the hill walking over a carpet of them to get to Diane's empty bird feeders? He, or she, comes every second night to knock the feeders about and to snuffle in the recycling box in which all the cans have been washed thoroughly. I guess it's just habit. A bear who once found easy food will place that spot on his or her regular patrol circuit.

Out in the woods an explosion of wild mushrooms is another sign of nature's generosity, and her dangers. Mushrooms flourish because of wetter than normal conditions. I've seldom seen so many different varieties and such spectacular colours. There were bright orange mushrooms, deep blacks, and brilliant whites.

Mushrooms have a mystical draw. You see one standing white and fleshy in a beam of sunlight illuminating the dark forest floor. It calls seductively: "Come over and pick me. I am delicious." I am tempted to pick and eat that mushroom. It looks so delicious, but I know better.

Cottage country bears do most of their raiding at night. But when the birdfeeders are full and the bears are hungry, they'll make daytime appearances.

Photograph by Jim Poling, the author's son.

I picked and ate many forest mushrooms years go. That was under the supervision of Emma Tadashore of Sault Ste. Marie, my mother-in-law, who directed me to pick only the little mushrooms that grew under pine trees. She would examine my harvest, then boil the mushrooms in a pot with a silver coin and a few cloves of garlic. That was back when silver coins still were made of real silver. If the coin and garlic did not turn green, the mushrooms were good to eat.

I've since read that is an old wives' tale. So now I don't pick any wild mushrooms, especially after reading a *New York Times* article in which a medical doctor described how he poisoned himself despite following a respected field guide to wild mushrooms. Apparently some of the differences between poisonous and edible mushrooms can be subtle. Ask Nicholas Evans, author of *The Horse Whisperer*, the popular novel that was turned into a movie starring Robert Redford and Kristin Scott Thomas. He picked mushrooms in the Scottish Highlands, cooked them in butter and parsley, and served them to his wife, brother-in-law, and his brother-in-law's wife. His wife and brother-in-law were placed on dialysis and wait-listed for kidney transplants. Evans received a new kidney from his adult daughter.

This reminds me that despite the considerable time I spend at Shaman's Rock I know too little about nature. I wish I had spent less time with my nose in computer manuals and more learning about the plant life around me, or the stars in the sky. I was forced to study computer programs to keep current for work. Now I wish I had spent more time studying botany, zoology, and the night skies. These subjects lead right into the reasons for, and purposes of life.

At any rate, the computer is low on my list of useful cottage tools. The connection speeds needed for modern computing aren't available in many parts of cottage country. That's a problem for many cottagers, but the upside is more time to sit back and watch nature work her magic.

As September advances, nature splashes her paintbrush on the hills around the lake. The greenery gives way to an eruption of autumn colours. Can anyone name all the different tones of colour? Persimmon, maroon red, bronze, tan, lemon yellow, scarlet, crimson, and cinnamon, old gold, winestain, tawny, and coppertone. The combinations are endless.

Fall colours bring busloads of tourists with cameras. With them comes much speculation, sometimes worry, about what is wrong with the annual transformation to fall foliage. Is the change of the leaves late this year? Perhaps earlier than usual? Are the colours brighter, or perhaps duller than usual?

Actually nothing is wrong. A late spring or severe summer drought can delay the autumn colours slightly, but generally leaves turn at roughly the same time and pace every year. What does vary is colour intensity. Temperature, sunlight, and soil moisture affect the intensity and duration of fall colours. Adequate moisture during the summer, and a dry, cool, sunny autumn are the ideal for the brightest colours.

Low temperatures above freezing favour anthocyanin formation that produces bright reds in maples. Early frost weakens the brilliant red colour and rainy and/or overcast days tend to increase the intensity of fall colours. Carotenoids — organic pigments — are always present in leaves and these produce the yellow and gold colours that are fairly constant in intensity from year to year.

The reds and bright oranges can be breathtaking in the bright autumn sunlight. The absence of high winds or heavy rain can prolong this autumn miracle of nature.

Most brilliant of all at Shaman's Rock is the young (thirty-year-old) sugar maple overlooking our lakefront. It is a fluorescent red. Just days ago it looked dull and we once again worried it would not show as the brightest tree on the lake. Overnight it has caught fire, a testament that whatever happens in nature little changes, or if it does, it changes slowly.

Competing with this sugar maple is the little burning bush that Diane received from a friend in the city and planted at the lake. It has taken to its new surroundings and now is afire with the shocking red hue from which it takes its name.

Some mums that Diane has nurtured add shocking yellow and reddish browns to her hillside wild garden. She has coaxed that hillside into a three-season flower garden that provides us much joy. It starts with crocuses peeking through the melting snow, followed by daffodils stretching and yawning in the spring sunlight. There are some tulips, when the squirrels don't dig up the bulbs. Later come the day lilies, poppies, irises, gladioli, purple alm, fox glove, hostas, and other flowers whose names I can't remember. Some of the last to give us some colour in the fall are the mums and the orange Chinese lanterns that look like little pumpkins hanging from the plant's branches. Then there are the hanging baskets with petunias and begonias, the latter which love the shade and give us spectacular displays.

Diane's hillside garden is a wonder, considering it started as a cliff. We dumped soil over it to transform it into a sloping hillside, then threw in seed. An old-timer at a feed store filled me a bucket of rye grass, horse meadow grass, clover, and other grasses and weeds that would catch and hold the hillside against erosion. Then Diane began digging through the mature grasses, bringing to life little patches that she coaxed into flower beds.

The colours of autumn are sadly temporary. By October's end, the burst of brilliance is gone, and with it the golden warmth of sunlight reflecting off the coloured leaves. We wish it could have lasted even just another week.

By late fall, only the most stubborn oak leaves cling to their branches, shakily resisting the first wind-lashed snowflakes of winter. The trees are stripped bare of leaves that now carpet the ground, already decomposing to fulfill their role in the cycle of life. This is when leaves are less entertaining. They need to be raked up from around the cottage and carted off. Left on their own dead leaves will jam eavestroughs, clog ditches and stain decks. Nature's plan for them does not suit the diligent cottager.

Cleaning up the fallen leaves can be back-breaking work. Eric and Bev Gilbert in the next cottage down the road rake leaves onto a large tarp, then drag it into the bush. We rake the leaves into piles and take them away in containers, wheelbarrows, or anything else that will work.

The unrelenting advance of power tools has eliminated much of the strain of gathering leaves. When the leaves fall on our lake properties we hear the roar of power blowers blasting leaves fifty metres into the bush. These babies blow air at 200 kilometres an hour or more, have electronic ignitions, cruise control, and variable speed throttles.

They also pollute the air and shatter the cottage country peace. Aching arms and back versus yet another noisy intrusion into cottage life? Everyone has to make their own choices.

— 20 —
CAMP COMAK

"The poetry of the earth is never dead."
— JOHN KEATS

Cottage folks watch out for their neighbours, including keeping a close eye on who comes and goes up and down the cottage road, and along the shore. So I was out of my hammock in a flash when I spotted a stranger poking along the road by my neighbour's place. He was craning his neck, peering around trees and bushes, and at something out on the lake.

I pretended I was out doing batting practice with my favourite Louisville Slugger and strolled over to see if he needed help with his neck. He was alarmed at first, then wildly apologetic, stammering an explanation of who he was and what he was doing there. He said he was from Seattle, visiting Toronto on holidays. I noted that Toronto was more than 200 kilometres due south through the bush, and you knew you were there when you spotted the top of the CN Tower and heard the gunfire from the street gang wars.

He stammered some more, and took a few steps backwards, pointed out to the lake and began blabbering about having spent childhood summers on St. Margaret Island. Finally his story all came together. He was a Toronto kid who moved away after university and often yearned to see the old summer camping grounds. So during his Toronto visit he rented a car, drove the three hours north and ended up on the St. Nora Lake road confronted by a guy with a baseball bat.

He was one homesick puppy. He talked wistfully about how every summer he was dropped at the landing on Highway 35 and boated across to Camp Comak on the island. They were the best days of his life, he said, gazing dreamily out to island.

Camp Comak summer camp for boys began in the late 1940s when a group of gentlemen bought St. Margaret Island and some of its buildings from the Woodruff-Band family. Private summer camps for kids had become popular in Ontario then. The first Ontario summer camp for boys was established in 1900 and popularity vaulted after the Second World War. Today there are hundreds of such camps in the province.

For more than two decades the voices of young boys rang across St. Nora Lake. The camp had tennis and basketball courts, athletic field, diving towers in the lake, an outdoor chapel, archery and rifle ranges, and a photo lab. Much was packed into a relatively small island, including the dog cemetery that had been established by the Woodruffs.

The camp closed in 1970 and the island was carved up into forty-three cottage lots that were sold off individually.

The guy from Seattle had gone to Camp Comak several summers during the 1960s. He was having a heavy nostalgia fit and was sincere and nice, so I put down the baseball bat and fetched the boat keys. I took him across the lake and we circled the island while he eagerly pointed out how the kids picked blueberries on that point and attended outdoor chapel on another point.

"Wow, the old stone pump house is still right there!" he exclaimed pointing at one of the island's more quaint features.

When the tour was over, his eyes were misty. I offered him some refreshment and lunch, but he said he had to get back to Toronto. He shook my hand extravagantly, offering numerous "thank yous," then headed back down the cottage road. I felt good about showing him the island almost forty years after he had last seen it. I often think about that guy and how many other people must have wonderful memories of their days at summer camps and family cottages.

— 21 —
ANOTHER VISITOR

"Since the house is on fire let us warm ourselves."
— ITALIAN PROVERB

Not long after the guy from Seattle wanders by, I have another visitor. This one does not make me feel warm and happy like the former Comak camper.

I'm having a late morning coffee when I notice a human shadow fall across a window. It's late fall and few people are at the lake, so you don't expect to find someone poking around your property. I go to the window for a better look and see a guy in khaki pants and a battered fly-fishing hat studying the cottage in detail. An old-style canvas book bag is slung from his left shoulder with the strap crossing the chest to the bag on the right hip. He has a pen in one hand and a notebook in the other.

He is an anachronism, standing there gazing at the cottage, then jotting down notes. With the canvass bag he reminds me of a British air raid warden in a Second World War movie. I see him move off to the woodpile and note that he seems impressed by neatly stacked insurance against a cold winter. He turns, approaches the door and raps softly. I answer like I hadn't known that he was there. He gives his name and explains that he has been contracted by my insurance company to check out the cottage.

Then it comes back to me: the insurance company had written me saying they would be sending someone by. They do this every decade or so to update their file on what they are insuring. The letter said I would not have to be there because the guy was surveying the outside and had no need to get inside.

Notebook still in hand, he asks if he can look around inside.

"Oh," I said. "The insurance company said no one needed to see the inside. In fact, I wasn't even expecting to be here today."

He turns and points to the woodpile. "Normally I don't, but when I see a woodpile like that, I have to look inside. You must have a woodstove."

I am gripped with apprehension. Insurance companies have created an atmosphere of fear not dissimilar to that which existed in Nazi Germany. People are afraid of them; afraid to lie, afraid to tell the truth, afraid that something they say will raise rates, cancel their policy, or lead to a claim being denied. The insured now feel that their interests are less important than the insurer's profit margins.

There is nothing to do, however, but face the situation. The insurance company is in charge and you do what they want or risk not being covered. I admit the visitor, who goes directly to the woodstove in the corner. He makes some notes, stuffs the notebook into the bag on his hip, then turns.

"I'm afraid your woodstove does not meet safety requirements," he announces. "I'm going to have report it as unsafe, but I can give you a few weeks to decide what you what to do."

That's it. The guy has condemned my woodstove, and if I use it the insurance company will refuse any fire claims.

I ask what's wrong with it. I explain that I installed it myself years ago according to regulations. I bought two sheets of galvanized steel and mounted them on the corner walls. I used pieces of copper pipe to hold the steel out from the walls, creating an inch or so of protective air space. The steel reflected the woodstove heat out into the room and away from the plaster board walls. Recently I had taken the steel down and had a mason do the entire corner in local red-grey stone, which looks terrific.

"The stone is the problem," the guy explained. "If you had sheet metal mounted as you explained, that was no problem. The stone is taking the heat and drawing it into the walls. After some years, you could take the wall apart and see that the studs would be charred black. You've done a nice job here, but unfortunately it's a fire hazard."

After some discussion, I concluded there were two choices: rip down the stone wall and put the sheet metal back, or replace the stove with a new zero-clearance model at a cost of $3,000 to $4,000.

I swallowed hard and called a professional installer who was certified and issued me the mandatory WETT certificate for the new stove, and a bill for $3,000 plus.

It was an expensive, but important, lesson. In most cottage areas the old days are gone. No longer can we throw up buildings or make modifications that do not meet today's rules and regulations. I'm no fan of today's galloping bureaucracies with their ridiculous fee structures, but ignoring their rules involves serious risks. Not following official codes for buildings, electricity, and fire can affect insurance claims and sale of your cottage property in future.

Like many things in modern society, you have to grit your teeth and accept it. It's probably for the best. There are no fire hydrants at the lake. The fire departments are volunteer brigades, which are fraught with their own problems, including lack of funds and volunteer exhaustion.

Fire protection is much the same as cottage road maintenance and insurance. You have to have it these days. In the old days if the cottage

Sketch by Zita Poling Moynan.

The winter cottager's best friend is the venerable and reliable woodstove. However, insurance companies have rigid rules for ensuring that cottage wood heating is safe.

burned, you could build a new one with scrap lumber and logs. These days, cottages cost tens of thousands — if not hundreds of thousands — of dollars to replace. If one burns down without insurance, it's not likely that the owner, if he or she is the average cottager, will be able to afford to rebuild it.

The guy in the khaki pants, fly-fishing hat, and carrying the old canvas bag was only doing his job. He did it firmly but pleasantly and tried to be helpful. He cost me much money and added anxiety, but he probably did me a favour.

Some contractor friends have convinced me that building permits, inspections, codes and other apparent bureaucrat regulations are indeed for our own good. Rules vary from one municipality to another, but the Ontario Building Code requires building permits to construct, demolish, renovate, alter, install, or change the use of a building. Some situations that require permits before a job can begin are:

- New structures greater than 10 square metres (108 ft²) in area.

- Additions to existing buildings or structures.

- Renovations that involve structural framing.

- Decks: new or replacement.

- Wood burning appliances: new or replacement.

- Replacement of windows or doors if the rough opening size is enlarged.

- Relocation or addition of plumbing fixtures.

- Replacement of water supply or drain pipes.

- Crib docks.

- Wind turbines that generate more than 3 kW of electricity.

- Permanent greenhouses, Quonset huts, and pre-engineered metal buildings.

- Replacement of piers under buildings.

— 22 —
BIG BOAT

"Trees and stones will teach you that which you can
never learn from masters."
— St. Bernard of Clairvaux

It is the perfect day; bright blue sky, not too chilly, with a slight breeze from the north. A terrific day to be outside, but I put on boots and fall jacket with sad reluctance. Today is the day I will take out the docks and the boat. The north breeze is exactly what is required for towing the docks south to the protected winter bay. The sun's summer strength has dimmed, but is strong enough to ensure that the boat can be put away dry.

I gather the wrenches and ropes I will need and descend the steps to the shoreline. The brightness of the day makes it hard to believe that I should be doing this. However, I am too old to be fooled. Too many times I have done this in the wet cold, even during a blizzard. Autumn is a talented actor. One minute it caresses you warmly and gently, seconds later it is snarling and throwing frost at your face and exposed fingers.

I untie the anchor ropes and put a wrench on one of the bolts connecting the steel hinges that hold the dock ramp to the shore deck. I know I will feel better about this tomorrow, or the next day, or whatever nasty day it is that will come to stiffen my fingers and redden my cheeks.

This is a ritual performed many times, but it still requires me to pay attention. Watch where you step, don't drop a bolt or wrench, pay attention to the process. A couple of years ago, Diane took a header off one of the docks, making an impressive splash in the icy water. That drew a laugh, until I noticed how close her head landed to the granite outcropping on the shore.

Our two docks are wooden floaters connected to each other by iron hinges and held to the shore by a three-metre-long and three-quarters-metre wide pressure-treated wooden ramp. Wrestling that heavy ramp onto the shore deck is the hardest part of the job. It takes two people to get the job done and we wonder how long we will be able to do this without more help. We have talked about going to an aluminum ramp cranked up by winch, but never seem to take it past the talking stage.

We built this dock system a quarter of a century ago. The first dock is a wood platform set on plastic drums. I built it out on the ice and used hand tools because there was no power on the cottage lot back then. Many of the older docks you see in cottage country are the same. They were put together quickly by folks with limited resources but eager to get something on which to place a deck chair. We are all the same we cottagers, hacking brush, pushing and pulling boulders, hammering nails, generally exhausting ourselves to achieve the ultimate goal: creating a spot on which to place a deck chair from which we can watch the wonders around us.

The second dock is bigger and has Styrofoam floats. We put it in when the family was getting bigger and we were running out of sunning and diving space. Much diving gets done here because the water is deep — five metres off the end of the dock.

Many cottagers prefer gently sloping sandy beaches but we have rock. Not boulders, but sheets of granite that drop off quickly. Not great for wading but excellent for diving. So far, all of our kids and grandkids have been swimmers who prefer diving straight in rather than wading.

Once the docks are free of the shore I tow them, one at a time, down the lake one-half kilometre or so to a protected bay. Here they spend the winter out of the current that moves the lake ice vigorously enough to damage any dock in its way.

St. Nora Lake is near the top of the Trent-Severn water system. Above us is Sherborne Lake which flows into St. Nora. The outflow is controlled by a small dam. Water is held back by this and other dams along the system. In the fall, usually right after Labour Day, water levels are lowered. Our shoreline late in autumn can be two metres lower than in spring.

If I bring the docks to the bay early, say mid-September, they are no longer floating when the water has dropped by November. The water is allowed to rise again when the ice melts and the docks are floating when I return to tow them back to their summer berths.

Once I am satisfied the docks are stowed securely for winter, I take a last spin around the lake. My boat, *Shaman*, always is full of spunk on this late season jaunt, happy to be let loose for one last spurt before the snows come. It moves spryly for an old boat, its 1985 seventy-horse Johnson pushing almost five-plus metres of aluminum hull made by Lund Boats Canada. It has served us well. The motor never has felt the cold grasp of a wrench, except for the one that changes its three spark plugs each year.

Diane is waiting at the boat launch on Highway 35. She has towed the old Easy Loader trailer over. I back it into the lake and then drive the boat onto it. The motor is still drawing water so I let it run. I take off the head cover, pull the fuel cord, and spray fogging oil into the carburetor. The old engine throws off clouds of smoke from the fogging oil, then dies. It has burned all the gas in its system and the fogging oil has given the cylinders a protective coating.

A quick wash and it is ready for storage. Later I'll drain the gear oil from the bottom end, watching to see if any water has leaked into the gear case, then fill it with fresh gear oil. Change the plugs, pull the battery out to storage, and *Shaman* will be ready to sleep until next spring. If the gas tanks have some gas, I add the required amounts of stabilizer, which keeps the gas usable for months.

We used to tarp the boat in the cottage driveway but that was problematic. I prefer to leave the canvas top up on its frame because shrinkage sometimes could make it difficult to put back in place. Just throwing a tarp over it was no good because St. Nora is in a snow belt and accumulating snow would crush the top's aluminum framework. So, we used to build a tent frame over which we would secure a large tarp. That was work.

A cross beam I used one winter was too light and the framework collapsed and seriously damaged the boat top. We later acquired a woodlot with large shed and now store the boat there.

With *Shaman* put away for winter, we are not without access to the lake. We have the small open "tin boat" with six-horse engine that I use for fishing. I keep it on the shore in fall until the snow comes. It is handy to take across the lake to explore the far shore, or nice to have handy in case some late boater needs a rescue.

Keeping an open boat can be problematic for cottagers. What to do about the rain water that fills it when you are not there? Dragging it in and out of the water is too much work in my opinion, so I let my little boat float all the time. I tried different ways of keeping the rain out: homemade cover frames, different covers. Nothing worked well. Many a cottage tin boat has gone to the bottom in heavy rains and it's a strenuous job to get dunked boat afloat again.

I bought a motorcycle battery and a bilge pump attached to a float switch. I screwed them to a board that I mounted on the floor at the stern. When the rain water floats the switch, the pump drains the boat, pushing the water out a plastic tube that hangs over the stern. It works well if I remember to give the battery a charge whenever rainfall has been frequent or heavy.

Watercolour by Jim Poling, the author's son.

Nana's Creek is a tiny watercourse on our woodlot where our cottage boat hibernates when the winter snows blanket the ground.

With the docks and boats put away, the sadness intensifies. Winter is a certainty now, just a matter of its length and its severity.

I check on *Shaman* and her winter berth one last time. She's scratched and worn in spots but I remember when she was shiny new back in the mid-1980s. Twenty-five years have faded some paint, but the aluminum is little touched by age.

I know some think a boat is not a boat unless it is wood. Aluminum and fibreglass, however, have extended boat life with much less maintenance than wood.

Lund was still building boats in Steinbach, Manitoba, when I bought *Shaman*. Then in 2006–07 the boat-building operations were moved to New York Mills, Minnesota, eliminating 140 jobs. I don't think the boats they build there now are as durable as the ones built in Steinbach.

Many people feel that way about many goods these days. The world seemed to start spinning faster with less attention to quality, and to service, late in the 1980s. The 1981–82 recession, and the effects that lingered long into that decade, changed the ways most companies operate. Quality and service had been taken for granted before then.

When I bought *Shaman* I noticed a small design flaw. I can't even recall what it was. I wrote a letter to the company in Steinbach where Lund had been manufacturing boats for more than fifty years. I wasn't looking for anything, just offering a suggestion for the future. They wrote back agreeing with the suggestion, and included a company cap as thanks.

Around the same time I was an active Air Canada frequent flyer. If service was not what I expected for the huge amounts of money my company was spending, I wrote directly to Claude Taylor, president of Air Canada. He personally answered every one of my letters. In later years I wrote a couple of times to his successors and never received a reply, or even an acknowledgment.

Times change. The world is more intense. Everyone is busier, always short of time. The focus of companies is on cutting costs to endlessly improve the bottom line. That is driven home to me when I visit Canadian Tire for a new container for *Shaman*'s spare gasoline. When I get back to the cottage I notice Canadian Tire sells gas containers made in the United States. They are marked in U.S. gallons, making oil mixing confusing because oil charts are in Canadian litres.

Also, there are no two brands of gas containers that use the same dimensions for spouts and caps. My shed is filled with a variety of gas containers, none of which is compatible. One of these days I'll throw them all out and buy one brand. Which, of course, is exactly what the manufacturers and retailers want.

Maybe that's just crabbiness brought on by the short days and approaching winter. Better to think about the fine service provided by *Shaman* over so many years. She has pulled her share of water skiers, and little kids on tubes. She is at her best providing summer pleasures. Sightseeing trips into Kushog Lake, quiet night cruises and visits to other cottagers. And, of course, the trips over to the rope swing where the kids can play Tarzan, swinging out over the water, then letting go. That was before government workers cut the swing down, presumably because it was close to an official camping site and they considered it a liability.

Water splashing, children laughing. Adults chatting or napping in the hot summer sunshine. Warm memories that help me hold on to another cottage season that is slipping away.

— 23 —
REFLECTIONS

"Nothing is more beautiful than the loveliness of the woods before sunrise."
— GEORGE WASHINGTON CARVER

The lake, dark grey and dead calm, awaits its inevitable transformation. The water is breathlessly still; waiting and listening for the approaching snow. The air is thin and chilly with introspection.

I am waiting also. I bundle up, perch myself on a slab of bedrock, and listen for the first sounds of winter. The ground is stiff from a severe overnight frost and the woods are so still I can hear my artificial heart valve clicking. There is no other sound, not even a breeze rattling the trees, which are cold and stiff in their nakedness. The leaves are raked, the outdoor furniture stored away from the elements. The outside water tap is drained. Fall chores are done and there is time for reflection, for taking stock.

My season's end reflection always includes a review of the Cottage Rules, those living commandments that make the difference between cottage tranquility and cottage chaos.

The Cottage Rules are many, and fluid, so much so that they have never been written down in full. There is an expectation that everyone should know them. However, some rules are so vital for peace, order and good cottaging that they are written down in a list called the Big Seven.

The Big Seven

1. *No tree shall be cut down without due consideration.*

2. *Nothing shall be flushed down the toilet that won't soften and start to dissolve within hours.*

3. *Males must remember to lift and lower the toilet seat.*

4. *No unnecessary noise before 9 a.m.*

5. *Work parties shall assemble for no more than three hours a day.*

6. *No horse play on docks or decks.*

7. *Granddogs shall be serene, not heard, and stay off beds and couches.*

I ponder deeply then conclude that, surprisingly, there was a high level of compliance this past summer. There was little unnecessary noise before nine a.m., which can be attributed to guests who were champion sleepy heads. Also, very little use of that soft and cuddly multi-ply toilet tissue that can slow the septic system. Single-ply might be a bit rough but decomposes much more quickly.

No breaches of Rule 5 concerning work parties. That one never causes problems, of course, except for the lobbying to reduce three hours to fifteen minutes.

Rule 3 concerning toilet seats requires constant reminders. However, none of my reminders are nearly as sharp as the one barked by Mike Jones, the bass fisherman, as a warning to his grandboys: "The next guy I catch peeing without lifting the seat is going to have his wee-wee nailed to the outhouse door!"

There was considerable controversy again over Rule 1: *No tree shall be cut without due consideration.* Some family members and guests, demanding more sunlight and open space, say there are too many trees and some must go without any more years of due consideration.

Rule 1 became cottage law in 1986 when Shaman's Rock was but a jumble of rock and trees. It was drafted to prevent the over-enthusiastic cutting that can turn cottage country into suburbia. It received unanimous agreement and the early years saw a few trees fall, but only in the interests of creating adequate space for building and some view of the lake. No other trees have been felled since, except those unfortunates that succumbed to drought, disease, or the ravages of chewing insects.

Each year there is much clamouring for a Rule 1 amendment to better define due consideration and make tree-cutting decisions more democratic. This would mean cutting trees to end complaints about the late afternoon sun being blocked from the dock. No longer would deck-sitters moan about having stiff necks from craning to see what's happening on the lake. I listen patiently, then veto amendments because I am Leader for Life and Keeper of the Chain Saw.

There is a powerful movement against cutting trees for cosmetic purposes. Cottage country municipalities are getting tough about tree removal, especially along shorelines with some forcing cottage owners to replant cottage shores stripped of trees.

A psychologist might trace my reluctance to cut live trees to early acquaintance with the whimsical works of J.R.R. Tolkien. I developed a powerful respect for trees when reading how his Ents of Entwood Forest marched against the Orcs during the War of the Ring. The Ents were strange forest giants, half-men, half-trees, who truly loved all trees and would not tolerate anyone harming them.

Some who want trees felled at our cottage say my refusal to cut is related to my notorious incompetence with a chainsaw. They rake up exaggerated accounts of the direct hit on the cottage utility trailer, or of the dead maple I dropped across the bow of my boat.

I never hesitate to cut trees that need cutting. Particularly those that have done their days on earth and can stuff a woodshed until it belches with satisfaction. I am a disciple of the late West Coast journalist Bruce Hutchison, who wrote in *A Life in the Country*, that a well-stocked woodshed is a humble miniature of a well-managed economic system. Wood to burn is tangible wealth.

The trees along my shore would be welcome additions to my woodshed. The lake view without them would be spectacular, allowing a panorama of the far shore cliffs reflecting the sunset. Late afternoon sun-tanning time would double. Besides, these trees are not always kind to me. They harbour gangs of thuggish squirrels who sneak into the dark branches to chatter shamelessly while plotting raids on the bird feeders.

The trees also shelter that really sick warbling vireo that lost its mind completely and took to warbling non-stop from four in the morning until long after dark. It made me crazy, filling my head with fantasies of defoliating the entire forest with Agent Orange. Also, these trees show no concern about their mess of leaves, needles, and cones that I must sweep from decks and docks. So the loss of a few will not tip the world's ecological balance. The chainsaw lobby probably is right that a quarter of a century of due consideration is a bit much.

Then I read about Diana Beresford-Kroeger, botanist and author of *The Global Forest*, who says trees are the most special species on the planet.

"Trees are the masters of the photosynthetic equation, plucking water out of the air, scrubbing carbon dioxide out of the atmosphere and in the presence of sunlight making sugars and releasing oxygen," she said in a May 2010 interview with the *Globe and Mail*. "We would not be alive without this."

"We've been given to understand that we're in charge of all things. But we're just the link. The pattern of intelligence in a tree is almost identical in chemistry to the pattern of intelligence in a human being.... In the ancient Druid legends, thousands of years old, people of learning said that trees have intelligence. So I think that, as scientists, we have to open our minds and broaden our thinking about what's going on around us. Because if the trees die, we die."

I don't know much about the science of trees. I do remember Tolkien's giant Ents who dedicated their lives to harmony in nature. My trees are like the Ents, sheltering creatures small and fragile, standing firm and tall to break the brunt of storms and blocking the scorching summer sun. Cottage life is trees and I accept once again that harmony in nature is more important than the likes and dislikes of cottage users.

— 24 —
HUNTING SEASON

"The woods were made for the hunters of dreams."
— Sam Walter Foss, American poet

So finally we meet up close and personal, the bear and I. He ambles up a rock ridge under the tree stand where I watch for deer. He looks around but does not have my scent yet. He is pre-occupied and has only one thing on his mind: food.

I am not in a warm and fuzzy naturalist mood, so I reach for my compound bow already loaded with a high impact killing arrow tipped with three pieces of surgical steel. The bears have driven me to distraction this year, twice frightening Diane, tearing down bird feeders that have been left empty, chewing inedibles like the kids' soccer ball and an empty watering can. They have left paw prints on the kitchen window and on my truck, and worst of all, have broken into my shed. It is time for action.

I raise the bow and sight it just right of the bear's shoulder blade. As I do my foot moves slightly, making a slight scraping sound. The bear turns, depriving me of a guaranteed killing shot, then saunters off in the never-ending search for food. The bush has lost all its leaves and I can see his glistening black coat moving away for thirty metres or more. I marvel how nimble these bulky animals are, and how silently they can move through the bush.

My son and I had agreed not to shoot any bears despite the fact that they had been prowling about the cottage, frightening anyone not familiar with them. They were here first and their only mission in life is to breed and find food. Also, it's not good form to kill things that you are not going to use. The locals up our way eat bear. I don't, so I'm reluctant to shoot one, unless it becomes a genuine nuisance.

It didn't take just this one, and a couple of buddies, to get high on the nuisance scale. The one that broke into the shed made off with a twenty-kilogram bag of cracked corn being saved for the turkeys during the hungry time of mid-winter. It pulled open a corner of the sliding, barn-type door and crawled in, breaking some pieces. The inside of the place looked like it had been tossed by an over-eager police crew on a drug raid.

The no-shoot pact was strained severely when bears twice trapped son Jim in the tree stand he uses to watch for deer. The first time, a large sow kept circling the tree stand area, unconcerned by shouts from above. Eventually it left. The second time, a bear arrived below Jim's tree stand late in the afternoon. It was still there when dusk began to fall. Jim had no intention of climbing down into the arms of a bear. He was reluctant to shoot it with his hunting bow and arrow for fear of wounding it, then sharing the darkening woods with an enraged bear.

I was back at the cottage worrying why he was overdue. The phone rang and his voice came in loud and clear from his tree stand thanks to the wonders of cell phone technology.

"Dad, I've got a bear here that won't go away. You better come up with a rifle."

I couldn't get in there on foot before total dark, so I took the ATV over a circuitous route into Jim's stand. The bear heard me coming and must have sensed I was unhappy enough to use the rifle. He left and we made our way out of the bush in the darkness without seeing it again or having to shoot it.

There is little discussion about whether to shoot a deer. Deer are plentiful, challenging to hunt, excellent eating, and cause problems to society, especially farmers and motorists. Burgeoning deer populations are defoliating parts of North America. Overpopulation of deer is so severe in some areas that the ecology is changing. Deer are ruining farm crops and cost the auto insurance industry and consumers millions of dollars every year. They also are responsible for many human road deaths.

Between July 1, 2008, and June 30, 2009, there were 14,117 deer-vehicle collisions in Ontario alone. For all of Canada, that number was 60,000.

Figures like that should chill everyone who drives to the cottage, and make them more aware and cautious. If you want to increase your chances of not hitting a deer remember to avoid dawn and dusk drives, use high beam headlights, scan both sides of the roadways, slow down, and remember that where you see one deer there likely are more. Don't rely on deer whistles mounted on your vehicle because their value has been questioned.

The autumn deer hunt only puts a dent in deer populations. In 2009, roughly 65,000 deer were taken by hunters in Ontario. No one seems to keep accurate counts on how many deer there are in Ontario, but recent estimates put the U.S. deer population at thirty million, up from 300,000 in 1930. Ontario populations dropped dramatically during the savage winters in 2007 and 2008 and with predators being at the top of their cycle. Biologists say the populations are growing again.

Fall for me always has been hunting season. I was born and raised in Northwestern Ontario and the wild woods always were not far outside my window. I've never been a fanatically serious hunter but hunting is in my blood. Just like getting next year's wood in March, there is an inner calling to go into the woods and hunt game.

There is little use my debating the issues of hunting in a modern, urban society. Hunting is inside me and debating it until the cows come home will not drive it out of me. Like the bear who feels an uncontrollable urge to find more food as the weather cools, I have an uncontrollable urge to go into the woods to hunt. I don't really care whether I get anything these days. I just have to do it. Everyone knows there is a large and vocal anti-hunting, anti-gun lobby out there, but that is a debate for people other than me. I hunt. Period.

My greatest hunting worry is about the people you find out in the woods these days.

There used to be a bush traveller's code under which goods could be stashed in the woods without fear of anyone taking them. Cabins were left unlocked. Boats and motors were unattended and unlocked.

The folks you met deep in the woods were much like yourself: They tended to mind their own business, respected personal property and other people's rights. More often now there are strange people found in the forests and odd happenings, some of them inexplicable.

In the fall of 2007, six people were held at gunpoint along an ATV trail just south of Shaman's Rock. They were ATV riding when they stumbled into a large marijuana grow-op. Twelve bad guys were there stealing the crop planted by another group of bad guys. The six citizens were held at gunpoint, robbed of identification and cell phones and generally terrorized for three hours. They were pistol whipped and even shot at before managing to escape. The bad guys were part of a large criminal group from the Greater Toronto Area.

A couple of years ago, I was walking the Dan Lake Road in the Frost Centre lands, poking about looking for partridge. The road is not much more than a cart track so I was surprised to see a two-wheel-drive sedan come bumping along the track. The car carried three men, none of whom looked like outstanding citizens.

The driver rolled down his window and we chatted, him eyeing closely my shotgun and commenting that it was a very nice piece. In fact, it is not a nice piece. It's an old, cheap, and battered Cooey single shot .410 that I bought when I was sixteen.

The guy in the back seat then jumped out and began approaching me. I didn't want to be unfriendly, but I backed up a couple steps because his approach was aggressive. The scene was beginning to look like one from the movie *Deliverance*. I moved my thumb onto the gun's hammer and the guy stopped coming toward me. He turned, got back into the car, and they all left without saying anything else. I was left with a real bad feeling about the incident.

Another time I was driving up the Sherborne Lake Road, a forestry track that heads east off Highway 35 into the Frost Centre lands. The road is sixteen kilometres long and at about kilometre twelve, a guy stumbled out of the snowy woods and flagged me down. It was late afternoon.

The guy was dressed for hunting and carried a deer rifle. He approached my window and explained that he was lost and needed a ride back to his truck. He didn't know which direction it was. I had not seen a truck while driving in, so guessed it had to be farther up the road. I didn't particularly like the looks of him but told him to hop in. I told him to put his rifle in the back of my truck, which he did, and kept alert. No more than a couple of hundred metres farther in, we saw his truck. He got out, collected his rifle, and left, still spouting his story about the horrors of being lost in the woods.

I went up the road a short piece, then decided not to hunt because it was getting near dusk and the snowfall was getting heavier. I turned around and on the way out I noticed his truck was gone. I stopped, got out, and followed his original tracks. They went down the road, then veered into the woods near where he had waved me down. Just inside the woods, he had sat on a stump. From the stump, his tracks went directly out to the road where he met me. He had not walked more than ten minutes from his truck. He had not been lost. He had been walking the road, then slipped into the bush when he heard my truck. He ran out and waved me down and presented his lost in the woods story.

You figure it out. I still haven't.

Neither have I figured out another bush mystery that occurred while out deer hunting alone on Black Mountain just south of Dorset. I drove up the Dan Lake track past Three Island Lake and bulled the four-wheel drive pickup through the trail up the mountain. I parked in about six inches of fresh-fallen snow and walked the other side of the mountain and down by Black Lake.

It was a fine morning; the new snow was pristine and without even a squirrel track. I hunted for about two hours and was returning for lunch on my same track. Ahead of me was a fresh track crossing the one I had made two hours earlier. I got excited but when I got closer, I was disappointed to see it was a man track, made not long before. It came out of dense bush, cut across mine on an old skid trail, then plunged into the thickest bush around and headed for a swampy area below the mountain.

I ate my lunch and decided to hunt another area. I drove my truck out to Highway 35, a distance of about seven kilometres, watching closely for man tracks or any other evidence that someone had travelled the road. Nowhere along those seven kilometres was a track other than my truck track. Whoever made the track walked in from the highway somewhere, travelling seven kilometres through thick bush to where I was hunting, then turned and carried on through the thickest bush in the area. By the time that person emerged back at the highway he or she would have walked a minimum of twelve kilometres through unbroken bush and up and down Black Mountain, which has an elevation of 1,250 feet above sea level.

The mystery walker was a genuine bushwhacker, and an anti-social one. Just before I spotted his or her tracks I heard brush breaking ahead of me. He or she knew I was there, but did not bother to stop for a traditional meeting and chat in the woods.

Recently, I was cutting wood on my bush lot on Highway 35 behind the cottage. I took a walk out to the highway for a break. At my open gate I noticed footprints that stopped, backed up, then turned left into the bush. A car was parked out the highway and I assumed the driver was just taking a little walk. I followed the tracks, one adult boot and one a bit smaller. They skirted the clearing where I was cutting wood and carried on through the woods. The snow was deep, up to my knees.

I went back to the cottage, dug out my snowshoes, and started into the woods to see if I could cut their tracks. I did. They had walked up a granite ridge and onto a trail that leads up to my deer hunting stand. The tracks went into the stand, circled it, then took off along the trail again. They veered off the trail and into the thickest part of my sixty-nine acres. I tried following, but the bush was just too thick to get through on snowshoes.

I backtracked, exhausted myself, and returned to the highway to find the car gone. I never did find where the tracks came out. Another bush mystery. Why would people slug through the dirtiest part of my woods after one of the heaviest snowfalls in memory? They obviously heard my chainsaw running and decided to skirt around me when they approached the gate. Someone scouting for an isolated spot to grow marijuana in the spring? Over-enthusiastic nature lovers?

Robert Service summed it up: "The arctic trails have their secret tales / That would make your blood run cold."

— 25 —
THANKSGIVING

"Nature is full of genius, full of the divinity;
so that not a snowflake escapes its fashioning hand."
— Henry David Thoreau

Shaman's Rock first came to life at Thanksgiving. Building started in September 1986, and by Thanksgiving weekend walls were up and the place was starting to look like a cottage. It wasn't habitable, but we decided to do Thanksgiving there anyways.

Aunt Terry and Uncle Gus brought up their motor home, which would be the Thanksgiving cook shack while Gus and I worked on the electrical wiring. Terry did up a turkey with all the dressings in the RV's small oven and eight or ten of us had one of the best Thanksgiving dinners ever.

After dinner I walked around comparing the building under construction with my Popsicle stick model. The previous winter I had collected Popsicle sticks and glued them together in the form of the cottage I wanted to build. It was a simple design that would see many changes over the years. It was basically a thirty- by twenty-five-foot box that provided two bedrooms, a small bath, tiny living room, and kitchen for a total of 750 square feet.

We wanted more space but couldn't afford it, so we designed a hip wall that raised the roof one metre to allow for a loft. This loft did not run across the back of the building like most. It was along the north side and gave us room for a couple of beds and some storage space.

A week or so after that special Thanksgiving, I moved into the place for weekend work. The roof wasn't complete so I draped a sheet of plastic over my cot in what would become the kitchen. The shingles had not gone up on the roof and the main door had not come in. I nailed a sheet of plywood over the doorway before I went to bed. The rain started and I watched it seep through cracks in the roof and down onto my plastic sheet.

About nine that night there was a knock on the plywood and a neighbour from down the road introduced himself (after I took down the plywood sheet and let him in). We had a beer and chatted. He left and I nailed the plywood back over the door opening.

There have been many different Thanksgivings at Shaman's Rock since, attended by many different people. One thing never changes on that long weekend: people come to cottages at the lake to savour the dying embers of another cottage season, and of course, to do final fall chores.

Thanksgiving can be a time of ownership changes in cottage country. Cottages often sell in the fall and at Thanksgiving you'll find excited new owners arriving to take possession.

This latest Thanksgiving there were unfamiliar vehicles at the first cottage on the road. Some possessions were being unloaded and the "For Sale" sign was being taken down. Halfway up the lake road, a family investigated the mustard-coloured former Brown cottage, which had been for sale for a year. We chatted with the people and learned that they were the new owners, just taking another peek before the deal closed at the end of October.

They are in their fifties and have adult children, typical of people who buy cottages these days. We were excited for them. Imagine the wonderful times they have ahead: outside picnics with children and grandchildren, quiet campfires, and much splashing in the lake. They have much to look forward to.

This cottage was owned for many years by the Vanstones. Audrey Vanstone was the daughter of Cec and Vi Davis who had the white clapboard place next door. They were fixtures at the lake and although I am happy for the new owners, I am sad not to see the old ones any more. Cottages change hands when owners grow old. I think of so many of the owners of the past. Mr. Winch, the Lehmans, the Malloys, and the

Browns and all of the others who enjoyed all that the lake country had to offer, but who gave much back to make it better. One of the lessons of cottaging is that the seasons of life are short and it's important to make the most of them.

When the sun is out on Thanksgiving weekend, so are the cottagers. They walk the roads and the woods, admiring the brilliant colours and breathing deeply the crisp fall air spiced with a tang of decay. These smells, sights, and sounds of cottage country will not be available to many of them until next April or May.

A Thanksgiving visit to Robinson's General Store in Dorset is man-datory for folks in our area. It's a neat place; a blend of old country store and modern supermarket. There's a real birch bark canoe hanging near the vegetables, a polar bear skin, some trophy trout, and a variety of hand tools used by lumberjacks in the old days. You can buy some chic clothing and souvenirs in the Red Onion upstairs. A section of old ceiling is still tin but the cash registers scan items and total your bill. The Red Onion name comes from the Red Onion Hotel that used to be on that spot in the lumbering days. In the 1980s, its customers voted it Canada's Best Country Store.

The Robinson family has operated the store since 1921. Harry and Marguerite Robinson worked in the store until their deaths in the mid-1970s. They were the ultimate locals. Marguerite was raised in Dorset while Harry came from nearby Bracebridge. Their son Brad worked in the store as a child and can still be seen hustling between the grocery shelves or the rows of hard goods.

His daughter Joanne and her husband Willie Hatton run much of the business these days and their son Ryan works there part time.

Dorset is a unique place because of Robinson's, and because it is the crossroads between Muskoka and Haliburton. The main street centreline divides the two regions and an old single-lane steel bridge connects the two parts of the main street separated by the narrows between Lake of Bays and Little Trading Bay. Sometimes kids can be seen jumping off the bridge into the refreshing waters below, while in late winter daredevil snowmobile jockeys run the open stretch of water beneath the bridge, hopeful of reaching the safety of the ice beyond.

Four hundred people live there permanently, served by a gas station, post office, a liquor and beer outlet, a couple of small restaurants, and, of course, Robinson's. On weekends, particularly in summer, the population can swell into the thousands. Brad Robinson says that 90 percent of the visitors to Dorset come from the Golden Horseshoe, the highly populated strip that runs around Lake Ontario from Toronto to Niagara Falls.

It might be tiny, but Dorset is packed with history. It was a centre for trade with the Indians, then it boomed with the lumber trade. That Gilmour scheme to run logs from Lake of Bays to Trenton filled its few streets with tramway workers and people employed in lumber industry support services. There were two hotels and two jails and steamboats stopped regularly at the dock by the Narrows.

Much of the history has faded into the background, but is being revived by some dedicated folks in the area. They have produced the Dorset Heritage Walking Tour, a booklet that guides you through a walk of the village, during which you can pause and recall that rich history. For instance, you might wonder about that old stone wall between the United Church and the post office. It was built originally to keep the livestock from wandering through the church yard.

Neat stuff. Thank God someone is trying to preserve and promote a piece of important Canadian heritage.

— 26 —
FROST CENTRE

"Fire, water, and government know nothing of mercy."
— PROVERB

St. Nora Lake rolls with the wakes of boats out for a final gallop before winter storage. Their last prance of the season takes them to a couple of ramp locations on the lake, and I can sense their reluctance as they are winched onto the trailers that will be their berths for next half year.

Shaman is nicely tucked away in its winter berth, so I hike out to the highway and over to the new concrete boat ramp to watch other cottagers trailer their boats. It's hard to imagine that after such an active summer at the lake, this ramp is about to go silent and stay that way until April.

The ramp and the little log hut beside it are part of the Frost Centre, most of which is mothballed. Haliburton Water Trails, a creation of Algonquin Highlands Township, has taken over the ramp and the log cabin is used as its office. Haliburton Water Trails now manages the trails and campsites throughout the substantial Frost Centre lands.

The new concrete ramp is a welcome improvement for some of us, but not all of us on the lake. Some people feel it will bring more boaters to the lake. They were coming anyhow, and the new ramp certainly beats the broken, rocky put-in trail that existed before.

It's busy at the ramp area, but quiet shrouds the other Frost Centre buildings, thirty in all I'm told, although I've never counted them. The complex, which for more than fifty years hummed with activity, has been silent all autumn, summer, and spring. It will sit through another winter empty but consuming our hard-earned tax dollars. I notice that some lights are on even during daylight hours, which seems odd considering the buildings have been empty for years.

The Frost Centre is an intriguing history lesson, and an even more intriguing lesson in party politics. It was established as a fire ranger base around 1921. The location was terrific. Just back from the edge of St. Nora Lake was a hill 1,250 feet above sea level on which a fire lookout tower was built, and below, at the lake's edge, a ranger cabin. When the Woodruff-Band family sold their mainland holdings to the University of Toronto in 1944, the little ranger station began to evolve into a forestry training centre. The current two-storey main building was constructed in 1945 and the Ontario government began classes there for trainee forest rangers and for fish and wildlife specialists.

The place grew in importance, becoming a main training centre for the provincial government. By 1974 it was important enough to be renamed the Leslie M. Frost Centre after "Old Man Ontario" Leslie Miscampbell Frost who served as provincial premier from 1949 to 1961. About then it began offering outdoors education to school children.

Just before it was closed in 2004, it had a new gun range for provincial law enforcement officers and an updated dining hall and kitchen to feed provincial employees and others who came for schooling and seminars. There also was a workshop, classrooms, sewage and water facility, and a main residence that sleeps 200.

The Liberal government of Dalton McGuinty closed the Frost Centre soon after being elected in the fall of 2003. Natural Resources Minister David Ramsay said the centre was not "a core function" of the new government and its closure would save $7 million over four years, money that could be directed to key priorities. Private assessments show that the savings actually were a few hundred thousand dollars a year. Now we have learned the same government has squandered millions of dollars a year on outrageous salaries and perks, the eHealth Ontario spending scandal, and questionable grants.

The Frost Centre sat vacant for about three years until a retired IBM executive, Al Aubry, got together some folks to start an environmental school called the Frost Centre Institute. It made a deal for leasing the

Frost Centre from the government, but the school closed in the spring of 2010 because of money problems.

"We just couldn't bring enough people through in the winter," Aubry told the media. Attempts to get the province to change the lease to a seasonal one to enable the Frost Centre Institute to stay afloat landed on deaf ears. Aubry said heating the facility during the winter months became prohibitively expensive at approximately $250,000 for the 2009–10 winter. He said the group tried to get a grant under the Ontario Development Program, but was turned down.

The Frost Centre sits on about forty acres of land that abuts more than 50,000 acres of Crown lands with established canoe routes, hiking trails, and ski trails. It sits on beautiful lake country that stretches off into many kilometres of interconnected lakes and forests right up to Algonquin Park. There are sixty-some lakes out there, 171 campsites, numerous trails, and seventy portages, making the area an outdoor recreation, education, and appreciation jewel.

The entire bundle is an incredible asset that screams "OPPORTU-NITIES!" Instead, it is seen as a problem by the Ontario government. There is a reason for that: the government is downtown Toronto, urban driven and has lost touch with life beyond the cities.

Thankfully, the people who worked to have the Algonquin region designated a park more than 100 years ago were not as urban oriented, nor driven by the dollar. They understood the value of Canadian heritage and the need to preserve it, especially during changing times.

But the Frost Centre sits empty, burning taxpayer dollars when it could be a viable training centre for government employees and an education centre for outdoor-impoverished urban kids. It could be earning the government some real nice coin as properly managed outdoor education centre.

Canadian governments and bureaucracies seldom exhibit the vision and spirit needed to successfully operate commercial/historical operations. An example is the history of Tom Thomson, one of Canada's greatest artists, and subject of one of Canada's greatest mysteries.

Some years back I had to get to the Algonquin Park gravesite where Thomson was buried originally. The little cemetery is on Canoe Lake, the water body in which he drowned, or was murdered, or whatever you think happened to him. To get there I had to be taken by a park official, a young man who knew the area from his teen years there. We had to go through a locked gate to get nearby. Then we had to find the path leading to the cemetery. It took some time for the young ranger to find the path because it was overgrown. We hiked the trail to the cemetery, which I gather has been saved from forest engulfment by a few private individuals who realize the significance of the place.

Similarly, I canoed the lake looking for a cairn built by the Group of Seven to honour Thomson. It was like exploring for Mayan ruins. I found an old dock, hacked my way through bush, climbed up a hill, and found it.

Compare this with the American approach to historic sites. If Tom Thomson had been American and Canoe Lake was in the U.S., there would be a paved road into the cemetery, which would be a national park. There would be clean washrooms, a museum and art gallery, and likely, hot dog vendors. We don't need a Tom Thomson carnival, but we do need a decent historical site at Canoe Lake.

About the same time I first visited Canoe Lake, I travelled through Kansas and stumbled across the village of Pawnee Rock, named for a huge chunk of stone on the flat landscape. There the pioneers stopped to rest on their migration along the Santa Fe Trail en route to settle the West. Names of pioneers were scratched into the rock and a small plaque told the story of the rock's place in American history. I learned that it was there that a young, still inexperienced Kit Carson shot his mule because he mistook it for a prowling Indian. Age and experience developed Kit into a much more adept scout, and of course, an American frontier legend.

Americans revere and manage the smallest pieces of their history. We have to search to find the historic burial place of Tom Thomson.

Places like Tom Thomson's final stomping grounds and the Frost Centre could be developed into valuable historic/education spots, which properly managed, could pay for themselves, provide much-needed services and even make a little for a cash-starved government. However, it's much easier and more profitable to expand government's ever-increasing dependence on gambling.

Shame on us.

— 27 —
THE ROCK

"Adopt the pace of nature: her secret is patience."
— Ralph Waldo Emerson

I stand atop Shaman's Rock and look out over the slate-coloured water that is flat and without a ripple despite the northerly breeze. The lake is stiffening, holding its breath as the cold squeezes the warm life from it. The first ice skin that will thicken to a depth of one metre or more by March will be visible within hours.

The freezing begins in the shallow bays and along the cold rocky shoreline, moving out to the middle of the lake. By morning the ice sheet will be a horizontal monolith that has obliterated the shoreline reflections that double the beauty of the lakeside.

The giant hemlocks on our shore seem unhappy that they will no longer be able to see themselves in the mirror of the lake. They are a much darker green, almost black in the slipping daylight, which makes them appear brooding, even angry.

The regal white pine that keeps guard over Shaman's Rock stands perfectly still in the transformation. It is such a happy tree, always alive with the movement of birds that seek its protection and the breezes rising off the lake to play with it. Now it is as stiff and quiet as the dark grey granite over which it has spread roots that have gone off in search of patches of nourishing soil.

Below it a reddish-brown leaf lies atop the water freezing at the shore. Soon it will be trapped in the freeze-up, consumed by the ice, never to be seen again. It will be many months before another living leaf appears to replace it. Then at this time next year, that new leaf will brown, and having fulfilled its destiny, perhaps fall onto the same spot along the shore.

The doomed leaf is the only hint of colour in a grey-white landscape that soon will be entirely white. Even the golden late fall foliage of the tamaracks is gone, pine-like needles having dropped. A strange tree, I think. A conifer that sheds its needles like other trees shed their leaves. The Indians loved it for its many medicinal qualities and because its wood was excellent for making snowshoes.

Four ducks paddle by, gabbling like tourists strolling a sun-splashed sidewalk in Paris. Then they lift off, quickly and without a takeoff roll, which tells me they are puddle ducks, most likely mallards. Fish ducks like mergansers skate across the water before taking flight. I wave, wish them a safe flight south, and wonder what has brought them here, and why so late. Ducks are not numerous at St. Nora Lake. It is a little too east of the Central Flyway for migratory birds. We do have wood ducks but they live in the wooded swamps beyond the ridge on the east side of the lake.

The ice is forming a bit later than usual. It has formed as late as January and as early as the start of December. It all depends on the weather patterns over the entire fall season.

One year the lake froze over on Christmas night. Snow fell as it froze and by morning the lake had taken on a mid-winter appearance. It was flat and firm looking, enticing for anxious snowmobilers who might not know better. Someone on a snowmobile scooted down to the landing used by the islanders, succumbed to the lake's enticement, and gunned his machine out onto its white expanse. He didn't travel far before crashing through. Luckily the ice was so thin that he went down in shallow water not far from shore.

It will be several weeks before the snowmobiles can risk the lake. The smart snowmobilers will check the ice thickness with ice augers and study the weather patterns before venturing out. There always seems to be an end-of-year thaw that can weaken the ice. One year the thaw came with temperatures as high as ten degrees Celsius and heavy rains that pummelled the earlier snowfalls and weakened ice, especially where runoff enters the lake.

Photograph by the author.

Cottages are about memories. The handmade "Poling" marker above the Shaman's Rock sign is an original from our first cottage at Mink Lake, near Eganville in the Ottawa Valley.

You wonder whether these wild weather fluctuations are manifestations of climate change, which is a serious and immediate threat. Or whether they are just weather anomalies that have always been with us.

There's not much conclusive evidence of global warming at St. Nora Lake. In the last sixteen years there has been only one record monthly winter high (plus twelve Celsius in February 1994). Two of the all-time monthly winter lows (minus forty in January 1994 and minus twenty-three in November 1995) occurred in the last sixteen years. The winters certainly don't seem to be unusually warmer, nor is the snowfall any lighter.

On the other hand, news reports indicate it is getting warmer in the Arctic and the ice is melting faster. A World Meteorological Organization report released December 2, 2010, said that over the past decade, global temperatures were the highest ever for a ten-year period — at 0.46 degrees Celsius above the 1961–90 average.

Our weather at Shaman's Rock might not seem to be consistently warmer or colder, but it does seem more violently changeable. The storms of summer and winter seem harsher. The December snowfalls are heavier and there are more tornados this far north in recent years. Environment Canada is hesitant to call them tornados, but twisting winds that uproot trees and lift roofs off buildings sure look like tornados to me.

Who knows what to think for sure about the climate change issue? Like many current issues, climate change information is clouded by twist and spin that makes it difficult to get the facts. Conversations on climate change are so polarized that it is difficult to form an opinion based on facts. Loud, dramatic, and angry is considered the most effective way of making your point these days. Drama queens and kings are everywhere, including the political theatres of Parliament and the legislatures.

Maybe spending more time observing nature would help bring thoughtful and reasoned debate to the grave issues facing our societies. Give some thought to the tree branch — how it grows and what affects its life — instead of just using it as a club to whack someone on the head to prove a point.

One thing I see in nature is its incredible ability to heal. Examples of this abound at Shaman's Rock. The lower trunk of the sugar maple in front of my deck has been rotten and hollow for fifteen years. It is the home of chipmunks who run up and down inside, occasional sticking their heads through decaying knotholes. Somehow nature has enabled that tree to bring its life-giving sap up from the roots and into its gloriously healthy crown.

Down Highway 35, there is little evidence of the uprooting done during that wild scheme to float logs to Trenton. Most people don't know that the ditch and swampy area just north of the Frost Centre and on the east side of the highway were a part of a canal in the great Gilmour adventure. There is barely a trace of the feverish excavation and construction that went on there more than a century ago.

Similarly, it is hard to find traces of the devastating clear cutting of white pine that occurred in the Canoe Lake area. When Tom Thomson arrived at Mowat on Canoe Lake in 1913 he saw the ugly wreckage wrought by the lumbering operations of the 1800s. Little was left of Mowat village except abandoned railway sidings, rundown sawmill works, abandoned logging and milling equipment, and barren sections of raped land strewn with wood chippings and sawdust. The mess of the former mill yard at Mowat covered more than twelve hectares. Today you would never know there was a town or any activity there. In fact, some people are trying to find and dig foundations to recreate what the Mowat site looked like at the peak of its activity.

The bush has been relentless in healing its wounds. Nature, given time, will consume all traces of any civilization.

No one would have believed in a recovery from the devastation of the majestic white pine forests that stretched from the Ottawa Valley through Algonquin to Georgian Bay. Now I walk the forest around Shaman's Rock and I see the hopeful signs. In every sunny clearing that gets good air, white pines have taken hold. One hundred years from now they will be like the giants that the loggers felled one hundred years past.

Mankind's things all decay and crumble eventually. Asphalt cracks and is broken apart by water, ice and soil that attracts the seeds that grow plants and trees that eventually cover it. Concrete weathers and steel rusts, and both sink into the soil. Nature is patient. She always recovers and wins, no matter if it takes years, decades, or centuries.

MANIDOO-GIIZISOONS

— 28 —
LITTLE SPIRIT MOON

"Tender snow-flowers noiselessly falling
through unnumbered centuries"
— JOHN MUIR, NATURALIST

I hear the snow falling. It is silent to my ears, but I hear it in my mind. One flake tumbling onto another, hundreds every nano-second, millions every minute. Building one upon another. *Thump, thump, thump*, like a heartbeat. My subconscious not only hears the snow, it sees it. It watches anxiously as it builds centimetre by centimetre on the deck railing outside my bedroom window. Like Pinocchio's nose, the pile on the railing grows and grows.

I can't stand it any longer. I throw back the duvet and push myself out of bed. My fingers hesitate at the switch for the outside light above the patio door. I flip it and my eyes are blinded by a white, swirling wall. Outside is the Storm of the Century. The accumulation on the rail has exceeded Pinocchio's nose, and is more than thirty centimetres high.

"We're getting out of here," I call to Diane who I have just awakened.

She mumbles something about it being four a.m. but picks up on the urgency in my voice and jumps from bed.

It is mid-December and this is the first serious snowstorm of the season. We are at Shaman's Rock without having arranged plowing, and our transportation is a two-wheel drive van, which soon will be rendered useless by this storm.

It's almost dawn by the time we have loaded our gear and shut the cottage down. The snow is just below my knees.

"You take a drive out to break the trail and I'll finish up here," says Diane.

"No trail breaking today," I reply urgently. "We have only one shot at getting out of here."

The drive out is frightful. The front bumper is pushing snow. I can't see the edge of the road, which is narrow at the best of times. The windshield wipers are working hard as they strain to slap away the snow, but they can't keep up with the rapid rate of fall. I turn off the headlights to stop the glare bouncing off the fat, fast-falling flakes.

We slide dangerously close to the ditch several times, but finally break out of the cottage track and onto the short piece of municipal road that leads into the highway. It is not plowed, but the highway is, meaning there is a one-metre bank of snow in our path. I gun the van and we hit the wall, which thankfully is soft because the snow is fresh and light and the plow has just been by. We push through the snow bank and onto the highway. A White Dawn escape from the Rock!

That was about the same time that Mel Lastman, then mayor of Toronto, was calling out the army to rescue panicked citizens and a hysterical news media after a moderate snowfall. He would have run screaming to get the U.S. army had he experienced the snow at Shaman's Rock!

We get two or three of those brutal snowfalls every winter. The worst now seem to come in early December before the lakes freeze. Warm, moist air over Georgian Bay forms into snow streamers that are blown east, picking up more moisture over Muskoka Lakes before making a direct pass over St. Nora.

Streamers turn our world white for hours, sometimes for two or three days. They can occur on clear days when the sun shining above the ceiling of snow looks like a clouded egg yolk.

Even on light snow years, there always seems to be a metre of snow outside our doors. The average annual snowfall at Muskoka airport, forty-two kilometres southwest of us, is 333 centimetres a year, or roughly eleven feet. I'm sure it's more at the lake. For instance, for the first eleven days of December 2010, Environment Canada reported that thirty-nine centimetres of snow fell at Muskoka Airport. That's just under sixteen inches. In the same eleven days I saw three snowfalls at the cottage, which I measured on the deck as almost 100 centimetres, or forty inches.

We don't run from the big, bad snowstorms these days. We stay and fight. We have an ATV with plow, various other snow fighting tools, and a four-wheel drive vehicle. The first part of the cottage road now is plowed, so we have little fear any more of being snowed in for the winter. Our area received more than 100 centimetres in two days in December 2009. The towns of Haliburton, Minden, and Huntsville were shut down. We arrived at the start of the storm and survived, although we did nothing but push back at the snow for three days. There's an urban legend that the Inuit have fifty different words for snow. I have two: deep and heavy.

The best part of a big winter storm is the aftermath. The sky, cleared of its depressing grey by a band of high pressure, is icy blue. Your nostrils pinch together in the cold and your ears hear the freezing lake moaning.

At night there are a million stars, and if you stand out on the deck and listen long enough you'll hear a wolf howl at the full moon. This is Manidoo-Giizisoons, the Ojibwe Little Spirit Moon. It is a small and icy moon, clutching itself closely, making itself small against the biting cold. No matter what night it appears in December, the Little Spirit Moon is the real start of winter.

Photograph by Diane M. Poling.

We used to fear the great cottage-country snowfalls until we bought a four-wheel drive. Snowfalls of forty centimetres are not uncommon at Shaman's Rock.

If we are lucky, the Little Spirit Moon sees the lake freeze over, followed by a stretch of clear weather with no snow. The lake becomes a giant's skating rink and we can strap on the blades and glide seemingly forever. We keep a couple of hockey sticks handy in case there are enough folks around for a game.

The most fun hockey was played with Gussie, the late big black Labrador belonging to Doug and Debbie Fraser, our cottage neighbours. Like all labs, Gus loved to chase sticks and balls, even hockey pucks. So I would get out on the snow-free ice and shoot a puck with all my strength. Sometimes it would fly across the slick surface out to the little island, Gus slip-sliding away in hot pursuit. There was no chance he would fall through because the ice was close to thirty centimetres thick.

This was my revenge for Gus's early morning summer visits. Each morning, just before seven, he would appear at the patio door and stare up toward my bedroom. I swear his staring would wake me up. If it did not wake me within minutes he would bark and knock his paw against the window.

I'd come down and slide open the patio door. He would give me a "good morning" look, then proceed through a hallway and into the back storage room. He would sit and stare up at a box of dog biscuits on the shelf. I would give him one, which he would consume with gusto, before proceeding to the firewood box in the living room. The firewood box was where we hid tennis balls from visiting dogs. Gus had figured out the hiding spot long ago, and pushed his snout through the firewood until he found a ball. Then, of course, he expected me to spend the morning pitching it for him.

Shooting the puck out to Woodruff Island and watching him slip, slide, and pant back and forth, was my way of getting him back for those early morning visits. It didn't take many shots before he tired and trotted off home for a nap.

It's not often that the lake freezes without snow following close behind ending the possibility of skating parties or pickup hockey games.

The arrival of serious winter weather always shocks. Winter never comes to St. Nora gradually. It comes straight from a standing start — zero to sixty in no time at all. Those last couple of late fall chores left waiting for tomorrow now will wait until spring. The hill terracing that I planned to widen is frozen and it's too cold to fasten those final two boards on the new decking at the lake. The best intentions die quickly under the gaze of Manidoo-Giizisoons.

— 29 —
WINTER WATER

"I had rather be shut up in a very modest cottage with
my books, my family and a few old friends."
— THOMAS JEFFERSON

It is a cottage morning ritual. I come downstairs and push the button on the coffee maker. Then I reach up into the cupboard and pull out my favourite clear glass coffee mug. Something is different. My sleep-fogged mind ponders what is different as I run the hot water faucet to get the chill out of the cup. Coffee is supposed to be hot so there is no use putting it into a cold cup, unless you are my wife, who puts an ice cube in her coffee.

My mind clears and the realization dawns. Cold cup from the cupboard. That means despite walls that are fifteen-plus centimetres thick and stuffed with heavy insulation, cold air is seeping into the building.

Cold cups and the recent arrival of the Little Spirit Moon tell me that winter is here. Little bits of autumn warmth clinging to life have been chased away. The trees outside the kitchen window are stark naked, cold grey in colour and devoid of any warmth. There is snow but the rocks are still showing, however they are cold to the touch, even in the late morning sun.

I shudder unexpectedly and remember that everything changes with the arrival of the Little Spirit Moon. There is no turning back. Life must be adjusted to cold that will deepen with each passing week until mid-March, and to snow that cannot disappear completely until the warmth of spring returns.

Folks talk of global warming and easier winters. There are no easy winters in Shaman's Rock cottage country. The average temperature is minus 6.6 Celsius in December, minus 10.4 in January, and minus 9.2 in March. The record lows for December, January, and February are all below minus forty Celsius.

Winter at the cottage is all about having an access trail path cleared and keeping the water running. It's invigorating, challenging and fun to snowshoe into a cottage, drill a hole through the ice to fetch water, and to transform a dead cold building back into a warm and happy shelter. Kind of fun once or twice a winter, but shovelling paths and drilling holes in the ice gets old quickly if you spend more than a couple weekends at the winter cottage.

We have a photo that reminds us what winter can be like at the cottage. It shows daughter Marcella and a girlfriend dragging a plastic bag of frozen weekend sewage waste down the snowmobile track from the cottage. Back then winter toilet facilities were heavy plastic bags over a bucket with a makeshift seat.

We love Shaman's Rock in winter, but it has taken years to develop a simple system to allow us to come and go relatively pain-free during winter. We've had to develop little tricks to prevent winter's quick and icy fingers from making life difficult.

For example, padlocks on sheds, gates, and chained possessions love to attract moisture and frost. Try inserting a cold key into a frozen lock in minus twenty Celsius temperatures. Too many times have we warmed a key with a match, burning fingers before loosening the lock. We cut up pieces of rubber inner tube to help protect padlocks from the snow and freezing rain. Sometimes even the rubber shield doesn't stop a padlock from freezing, so my parka pocket always holds a small bottle of isopropyl alcohol or methyl hydrate to splash into a lock.

We tried heating Shaman's Rock full-time for two or three winters. We set the electric baseboard heaters just above freezing. That little bit of heat kept the deep cold out of the place and made for a quicker warm-up whenever we arrived back.

Power rates are too expensive for that now, so we leave most of the building unheated. A dead-cold building takes much more time to heat.

We find it takes twenty-four hours to drive every spot of cold out of the woodwork and to get to a steady t-shirt temperature. The woodstove has to be worked hard to achieve that, and the woodpile takes a beating. I sometimes wonder if it isn't better just to pay for the power and save some of the work that goes into keeping the woodpile flush.

Frozen pipes, of course, are a serious worry, and each cottager has to work out a prevention system that works best for them. Every cottage is different in exposure and how it reacts to cold. Experience, experimentation, and a few frozen pipes usually lead to a relatively freeze-proof system.

I could never figure out why my hot water line always froze when the cold did not. The layman assumes the cold should freeze first. The experts argue about why the hot often freezes before the cold, but can't agree on the reason. My best guess is that hot water evaporates a bit even inside a pipe. There is less water in the hot water pipe, so it tends to freeze first.

Theories don't matter. It makes little difference what freezes first. You don't want any pipe to freeze because unthawing them or repairing them after they burst can be nasty work.

I set myself afire once while trying to repair a burst pipe. It was the dead of winter, brutally cold, and the burst pipe was located in the floor joists at the edge of north wall of the cottage. I crawled under and started the repair. I had to adjust something and set the blow torch in the snow beside where I was crouching. I was busy working away when I felt a sharp, hot pain in my hip. I assumed it was from the way I was positioned under the cottage. It got more intense. Then I smelled fabric burning. I looked down and left leg, hip, and back were on fire.

I rolled in the snow at the edge of the cottage, then threw myself out over the hill, rolling down toward the lake in the snow. When I got the flames doused I realized that the lighted torch had tipped over and set my heavy winter overalls on fire. I had cherry-red burn on my hip.

When we leave the winter cottage we drop the water from the distribution lines by closing valves at the pressure and hot water tanks. That way there is no water in the pipes except at the two tanks, which are in little pump-storage room that we keep lightly heated. We open the two valves and flick a switch to get the water back to the sinks, toilets, and showers.

179

When there is a chance that electrical power might fail in weather minus twenty Celsius or lower, and we won't be around for a week or more, we drain all the water, including that in the pressure and hot water tanks.

The difficult part of the winter water system now is getting other family members to understand it. I can bring the water up and down in my sleep, but others find the system complicated.

There is always something that can screw up the system. Before you drain any water, you want to make sure the water tank electrical breaker is off. The heating elements in the water tank burn out quickly if they receive power when the tank is empty. I always make sure hot water runs from the faucet before I turn the hot water breaker on.

You have to be firm about instructing people what not to put down a sink drain or toilet in winter. The rule about only single-ply toilet tissue, body waste, and water going into the waste system is an especially important rule in winter. If something snags in the waste pipe running to the septic system it can freeze and start a backup. Before you know it you have several feet of solid ice in the waste pipe.

It happened to us once. I tried everything to thaw the pipe, including driving to a hardware store to buy electric cable to wrap around the waste pipe. All attempts failed to get the pipe thawed. Then Diane's mom called from Sault Ste. Marie and Diane explained that the cottage sewer system was frozen and we were trying to find a way of thawing it.

"That used to happen to our house in the old days," said Diane's mom. "Pour a quart of methyl hydrate into the sink and the ice will be gone by morning."

Our waste pipe was backed up and frozen for four metres. It seemed impossible that pouring in a bit of methyl hydrate would help. We were desperate. We drove to town, bought a quart of the stuff, and dumped it in the sink and went to bed. At dawn I got up, crawled under the cottage and tapped the pipe. All I heard was an echo. The pipe was clean as the proverbial whistle. Another lesson learned by listening to someone who had done a lot of living in tougher times.

Once you develop some methods to push back at the cold and snow, winter cottage living is spectacularly restful. In the mornings you can sip coffee and watch the blue jays, chickadees, and nuthatches at the feeders, and below them, the daily troupe of wild turkeys. At night you can sit reading, or lie in bed, listening to the lake ice expanding and cracking, the thunderous booms radiating up the hill through the bedrock and into the cottage foundations. At other times you hear the roar and screeching of ice packs loosening and sliding off the roof.

Canada's roots are deep into the bedrock. Winter in cottage country is a reminder of what this country is and what its people had to do to develop into a modern society. It is a reminder that although Canada has become an urban society, there are still tens of thousands of its citizens who live on the fringes in harsh conditions. They haul wood and they haul water, and they don't have high-speed Internet, Wi-Fi or cell phones.

It's easy to forget that when you sit in a winter cottage supported by modern technologies and conveniences. It's even easier when you sit in taxpayer-supplied surroundings at Toronto's Queen's Park. None of us ever should lose track of how people live in the forested fringes.

Nor should we forget the importance of independence and individualism in building this country. In cottage country and beyond, no one needs government to tell them how to tack a piece of inner tube over a padlock to make sure it works in winter.

— 30 —
ALONG CAME LORNE

"Winter lies too long in country towns; hangs on until it is stale
and shabby, old and sullen."
— WILLA CATHER

I've only met Lorne Heise a couple of times, but I love the man. He represents cottage ingenuity, and he's the guy who delivered us from the horrors of Screaming Saturdays.

Screaming Saturdays had to do with our original water system. The system was typical of cottages twenty or thirty years ago. It consisted of an under-the-cottage jet pump that drew lake water through black plastic pipe into a pressure tank that pushed the water through the cottage plumbing.

The water line had to be disconnected and drained for winter, then reconnected and put into the lake after spring ice out. Some people avoided this ritual by using plastic water pipe with a copper heating element running through it. This prevented winter freezing, but if these lines lost water when the element was on the pipe might burn through. Also, if covered or insulated they sometimes overheated and burned out.

Screaming Saturday at our place was that weekend in spring when the water line was reconnected. Clean the water line foot valve, make sure it was not cracked, then get into the boat and drag the line out and sink it in deep water. After that, climb into the pump room under the cottage, attach the water line to the jet pump with O clamps, then begin the horrors of trying to prime the line enough to start drawing water. Air locks, leaks, foot valve problems — all sorts of things always prevented a proper prime. Screaming Saturdays often continued into Screaming Sundays with tools flying, profanities being shouted, and hair being pulled out.

Lorne Heise changed all that. He invented a water line heating system called Heat-Line.

Lorne was the local electrical guy, operating Carnarvon Electrical Contracting Ltd. out of his place at the bottom of Kushog Lake, which is joined to St. Nora Lake by a shallow narrows. Also, he was a pilot and had his own float plane, which he sometimes used for calls.

In the early 1980s, Lorne was intrigued by the possibilities of making winter water more easily available for cottagers. He often was called upon to fix broken or burned out heated lines, and figured there must be a better way to prevent water line freezing. He played around with ideas, did some experimenting and invented a prototype water line that had heating elements imbedded in it and was self-regulating. In other words, the heat cable came on only when the water was close to freezing.

Then one day just before Christmas he was eating a spaghetti dinner when the telephone rang.

"The cottager calling had one of my prototypes. The line ran over rock and he was not getting a full flow of water."

Lorne went back his spaghetti, then it struck him. He called the guy back, told him to cover the pipe, and lo and behold, the freezing stopped and the water ran as it should.

"That was a huge moment. That's when we realized we really had something."

He had invented a better heated water line. But no thought had been given to insulating. That day showed him that his Heat-Line could be heavily insulated without ever overheating, meaning that less electricity would be needed to prevent freezing.

In 1988 he founded his Heat-Line company. He opened an assembly plant adjacent Stanhope Airport over by Haliburton. Now he has a research and development facility there. The company has expanded its horizons beyond cottages. It makes freeze protection systems used in railway systems, transport trucks, RVs and fire department trucks. It has invented ArcticVent, which is designed to protect plumbing vent stacks from freezing in temperatures below minus fifty degrees Fahrenheit.

Also, he has invented the Limnion Lima-1 geothermal transfer system that takes energy out of water and uses it for heating, or cooling.

This is a ball-like device containing 1,680 metres of small plastic tubing. Two people can set it into a lake, river, or pond. It connects to a heat pump that will heat or cool a cottage or other building.

Transfer of energy from water is not new but until now has been done with huge sunken rafts of black water pipe. The Limnion system is dramatically smaller, far easier to install.

I heard about Heat-Line from mutual friends when Lorne was just getting it on the market. It made complete sense to me and we put it in. Now we have water all winter and the line is connected to a thermostat that helps save electricity. It runs through black insulating pipe out of the cottage and down the hill to the lake. Because we are on bedrock, much of it is exposed.

A couple times in winter I arrived to discover the outside line frozen. No water! Just what I had tried to avoid. I quickly learned that I had set the thermostat too low. I turned it higher and within an hour I could hear small chunks of ice clanking their way through the line. Not only did Lorne's Heat-Line prevent freezing when you set it properly, it quickly thawed a line that froze when you didn't.

Sometimes I spot Lorne's yellow float plane flying low over our lake. I always wave because he made cottaging much easier and enjoyable for a lot of people. And, he has provided hope because much of the stuff he has invented has helped lessen our impact on the environment.

It's really neat that a local guy living just down the lake did all that.

— 31 —
PREDATORS

"When I hear the coyote wailing to the yellow dawn, my cares
fall from me — I am happy."
— HAMLIN GARLAND

December can be a busy time along the mouse trap lines. The tiny
pests begin infiltrating in late fall, looking for a warmer digs inside
the cottage. This is a time for vigilance and for making sure the mouse
bucket is in top operating order.

This year, oddly, there are few signs of mice migrating from the
outside cold. The mouse bucket has been refreshed a couple times,
fresh gobs of tantalizing peanut butter slathered along the bottom of
its tricky rolling stick. No takers in weeks. The spring traps Diane has
set up in the laundry room as an early warning system have remained
silent and unsprung. One little black mole did wander into Diane's
minefield and got its tail caught, but no mice have shown.

The talk at Robinson's Store and Dorset post office is that this is a
low year for mice. People note that owls, night hunters, have been seen
hunting in daylight because prey is scarce. Red squirrel raids on our bird
feeders have been few. And the chipmunks, whose frenetic antics below
the feeders amuse us greatly, became fewer even before the snow came.

The animals we see this year are mostly the big ones, which is not
the norm. There are more moose. Several have been seen at the cottage. And need we mention the bears, which have been more present,
and peskier, than any time in our twenty-five years here. Raccoons,
usually always poking about at night where there is free food, are not
as plentiful.

We have seen something very unusual — more pine martens, those fast and ferocious members of the weasel clan. They have been patrolling the area below the bird feeders, where spilled seed has attracted mice, chipmunks and other critters small enough to make a meal for a hungry marten.

Add to these observations more sightings of wolves and coyotes. Whenever you talk with someone in town, the conversation quickly gets to stories about wolf and coyote sightings. There have been two timber wolf sightings in daylight near St. Nora Lake recently.

All this points to predators being at the top of their population cycle. Erin MacDonald, Ministry of Natural Resources biologist at Bancroft, mentioned that to me in 2010 when we visited a deer yard to gather some observations on how the deer had wintered. There were fewer deer in many parts of the province, part of which is attributable to those two severe winters a couple of years back. Erin said predator populations are

Chipmunks are the most welcome animals at Shaman's Rock. They are content eating the seed that spills to the ground from the bird feeders. They are busy and curious, but seldom raid the feeders or try to get into places where they are not wanted.

Sketch by Zita Poling Moynan.

high but will begin to fall. It's a supply and demand situation. As deer and smaller critter populations fall, so will the numbers of predators who feed off them.

There are more predators in established cottage areas than most people think. They almost always stay to themselves, shy of people and people things. They will snatch small dogs and cats, maybe even a little kid rarely, if they get an unchallenged opportunity. Which is the reason for an important rule at Shaman's Rock, and a good one for any cottage: don't leave smaller domestic animals or little kids out of your sight. The windows at Robinson's Store, where people stick personal advertisements, sometimes are cluttered with notes pleading for news or sightings of little Bowser or Hector the cat, who have gone missing. There's not much use posting the notes unless coyotes and wolves take up reading.

Few things are more exciting than seeing a wolf in the wild. Fewer things are more chilling than being in the woods alone and unarmed, and finding evidence of a wolf nearby.

One sunny blue March morning I snowshoed across St. Nora Lake and entered the bush near one of the summer camp sites. I was out for the exercise, the air and beauty of the morning. Just beyond the tent site was an intriguing cut that climbed up between two granite walls. It looked inviting, so I decided to explore. Near the top of the cut was flat area with a copse of hemlocks much thicker and darker than the rest of forest. In front of me in the fresh fallen snow was the largest wolf track I have ever seen. It led straight into the hemlock thicket.

I'm not an expert in animal tracks and signs, but I do know a fresh timber wolf track when I see one, especially when it is in new snow far from any human development. My heart quickened and my bowels loosened. I've never before been in a place in the bush where I felt I didn't belong, or where I felt so vulnerable.

I turned on my snowshoes and sidestepped back down the cut, keeping my face turned as best I could toward the copse. I know that wolf was in there, watching with yellow-brown eyes and weighing his options. I kept thinking about the 1946 short story *The Pursuit of Peter Bellise* by American Robert Murphy, in which a Métis hunter is pursued by a wolf pack.

I often wonder what might have happened had I gone deeper into that wilderness across the lake where the wolves howl regularly on winter nights.

J.W. Curran, founding publisher of the *Sault Ste. Marie Daily Star* in 1901, wrote a book in 1941 called *Wolves Don't Bite*. He offered a reward, as a promotional stunt, to anyone who could prove they had been "et by a wolf." The *Sault Star* was my first newspaper job, so I always had faith in what he had written. It was a shaken faith, however, as I hustled my way out of the woods that day.

Ministry of Natural Resources biologists estimate there are only 8,000 wolves in Ontario, and one for every 100 square kilometres in central Ontario. In Algonquin Park, not far from Shaman's Rock, there are three for every 100 square kilometres.

That's not many wolves when you think about it. The chances of seeing one are slim, and chances of being eaten by one are pretty much nil. Still, there have been sightings around our cottage. I have seen several, but in each case the wolf had broken cover during the heat of a chase.

Coyote sightings are another story. Sightings are daily talk throughout much of the province, even in the cities. Farmers complain of losing more chickens and more sheep to wily coyotes.

The coyotes we have in Ontario are a cross between the western coyote and the eastern wolf. They look larger than they are — they weigh roughly sixteen kilograms — because they have a thick coat and bushy tail. They have adapted to urban environments since moving in from the west more than one hundred years ago.

The much-debated question in our part of cottage country these days is whether cougars exist outside of western Canada. The Ministry of Natural Resources says it has collected more than thirty pieces of evidence, including tracks, DNA, and scat that verifies that the wild cats do live in Ontario bush lands.

"Cougars have been here all along ... we are collecting additional information about them now," Rick Rosatte, a senior research scientist in Peterborough, told the *Toronto Star*.

Cougars definitely existed in Ontario in 1800s and the last report of one being hunted and killed was in Creemore, just south of Collingwood, in 1884. The Ontario Puma Foundation says the animals never completely disappeared. Their number dwindled to a low of about forty, but now the foundation estimates the Ontario cougar population at 550.

There have been approximately 2,000 reported cougar sightings in the province since 2002. Few have been confirmed by track marks or DNA.

What's interesting is that with all these sightings, estimates of 550 cougars and various investigations, no one has produced a cougar. The ministry has set up trail cameras but has not produced one photo of a cougar. Also, there has never been a confirmed attack on a human by a cougar in Ontario.

Some people up our way say the government has released cougars into the wild to control deer populations. Others say they have seen the big cats in the forest.

All I know is that there are more predators out there. More wolves, coyotes, and smaller meat eaters. I also know that will change. Nature keeps things in balance, one way or another.

— 32 —
DEATH ON THE ICE

"There are, of course, several things in Ontario that are more dangerous than wolves. For instance, the step-ladder."
— J.W. Curran

Son Jim is making morning coffee in the kitchen and glances out the window overlooking the lake. What are those two dogs doing so far out on the lake, he thinks, especially when the ice is not fully formed. It is the Christmas–New Year holiday after a late autumn and not enough bitter weather to safely freeze the lake. No cottagers are on St. Margaret Island because of the thin ice, and the snow machines are still under wraps awaiting colder weather.

Jim pulls out the binoculars and sees that those animals are not dogs. They are wolves padding across the thin ice on wide, snowshoe-like paws. They are on a serious mission: running down a terrified female deer.

They had chased her out onto the ice, a favourite wolf tactic. Her sharp hooves on slick ice over an open area are no match for those padded paws. The thin ice gave out under her and down she went. She struggled hard and got her front legs up on unbroken ice. As she struggled to get out, the wolves closed in. They worked as a team, taking turns running at her and nipping her neck.

The deer was bleeding and weakening. The weaker she got, the bolder they were at lunging at her and tearing away pieces of flesh. Jim watched through the binoculars as, finally, her head slumped and did not raise again.

The drama on the ice played out for one and one half hours. There was some debate over whether he should let his two children, roughly nine and eleven at the time, view the scene.

"He wouldn't let us look, but then he did," recalled Jessica, the eldest. "We could see the blood on the ice. I kept telling my dad to go out and save it."

She pleaded with her father to get a rifle and walk out and shoot the wolves. He explained that the ice might not hold him, and if he shot the wolves he would still face the impossible task of pulling a dying deer from a hole in the ice.

"I was traumatized," said Jess. Her brother, Robert, got his turn on the binoculars and was mesmerized by the scene.

It was a brutally ugly scene, but one that needed watching. We are in the bush here, surrounded by nature, and where life and death struggles play out every minute. This is not the Cineplex, nor a video game. This is a place where every action creates a reaction; a place where animals, insects, birds, fish, and even plants must kill to survive.

More recently we had a similar happening and I felt terrible about it because I was in a way responsible for it happening.

Snowfalls had been huge, far above average, and animals were struggling to get food. Turkeys, then deer, began coming to our bird feeders for seed spilled into the snow. One deer discovered that the easiest route to the feeders was across our shovelled deck. But to get from the deck, she had to go down a narrow set of stairs. I studied her tracks one day and realized that her right hoof had missed a step and plunged deep into the snow. I didn't think much of it, until a day or so later a cottager up the road reported seeing a deer with a broken right leg.

Then the neighbour reported seeing the same deer, bleeding from the face and neck, fleeing past his window. In pursuit were two large, black wolves. They took her down as she struggled through the deep snow on a wooded ridge, and we walked in later to see her remains.

Talk of such scenes sickens some people. They are sad, but real, and part of nature. These animals hunt and kill stay alive. What sickens me is that in our cities people hunt and kill each other for no reason at all. That is not natural.

— 33 —
LITTLE BOY LOST

"Nobody ever expects to get lost, but it happens."
— U.S. Search and Rescue Task Force

The wolves and coyotes and cougars, if indeed there are any out there, missed a first-class dinner opportunity at our place some years back. We had a little kid go missing at our cottage in winter, and predators or not, it scared the hell out of us.

Mid-winter is usually a time when adults can lighten up cottage kiddie vigilance a bit. I mean what can happen in winter? The lake is frozen solid. The snow is too deep for wandering off. But one day while we were all working and playing outside, grandson Robert, then four, vanished. Poof, into thin air.

Diane and I had been asked to look after Robert and his older sister, Jessica, for the weekend. What better place to take them than the cottage. We could build snow forts, have snowball fights, start a winter campfire, and all that fun stuff. The fun stuff was put on hold when I decided to take down a dead oak along the shoreline. What better time. Drop it onto the ice, buck it up, and bring the rounds up for firewood.

Diane and the kids played on the ice while I cut up the tree. We all hauled the pieces up from the ice. We set the last piece on the pile at the cottage when someone asked, "where's Robert?" He had been right there beside us, not two seconds ago. Now there was no sign of him. The snow was too deep for a toddler to walk through. The road was unplowed and the only way in or out was on the snowmobile track.

I ran down the snowmobile trail, calling for Robert. No reply and no evidence that he had been on the track. It was like he had been carried off by an eagle.

Panic started to set in. We considered ourselves diligent cottage grandparents, so diligent that in the pre-grandchild era we spent hours discussing ways to make our cottage totally child safe. Now we had a grandkid lost in ten million square kilometres of Canada at its Arctic best. How did this happen?

Between stabs of panic, there came a clue. Freezing rain had crusted the snow the day before. Although the rest of us crashed through to our hips, Robert walked on top. It became chillingly obvious that a kid walking the crust could cover more territory at a faster clip than in summer.

No one could say exactly how long it had been since Robert slipped away. It must have been ten or fifteen minutes. Constant shouting and a complete inside cottage search produced nothing. We fanned out into the surrounding wilderness. Another fifteen minutes passed, producing tears and heart palpitations.

It was time to call the police. Then someone, likely Jess, got a grip and realized their dog Emma, a big loving brown Labrador, also was missing. Maybe the boy and the dog were together. We decided to continue the search for another fifteen minutes before calling the police.

I walked the snowmobile track hoarsely bellowing "Emmm-maaa!" "Robbbb-ert!" About half a kilometre from the cottage I heard a little voice back in the woods commanding "No, Emma, this way." I plunged into the deep snow, pushing my way up a hill, when at its crest appeared an elf-like apparition in moon boots, toque drooping over his eyes, and scarf dangling to his knees.

Robert stared down with an incredulous look reserved for adults who overreact to the simplest situations. His reply was matter of fact: "I went looking for Emma. I think she was lost."

I turned to Emma, who in her years as senior cottage granddog had never wandered beyond sniffing distance of her dog biscuits. I thought I saw her rolling her eyes, but probably just imagined that.

There is a lesson in this: never, ever, under any circumstances let your eyes off a kid at a cottage. It must be clear to every adult at the cottage that one person at all times has to be designated to keep an eye on the kids and to ensure handoff plans are clear and well communicated.

I am obsessed about this, and have been since I was a young reporter in Sault Ste. Marie where I covered a two-day search for a toddler missing at a cottage. No one could find any evidence of where the kid went, until one searcher looked under a dock and found the child floating face down in a dark, hard to see spot. The child had not been neglected. It had strayed, slipped, and disappeared while heads were turned.

And how will I ever banish from my head that image from the St. Mary's River in the Sault? I was with a police officer looking for a nine-year-old girl missing from a house across the street from the river. We climbed over high snow banks and found a hole in the ice. A pair of mittens were frozen to the side of the ice hole. The child had fallen through the hole and clung to edge while calling for help that never heard her. Then she slipped out of her mittens and drowned.

Not all accidents, even tragedies, can be avoided. The best way to try to prevent them is to be obsessive about keeping eyes on kids. They don't have to be smothered, and they don't have to know you're watching, just as long as you are.

— 34 —
ICE FISHING

"In the depth of winter, I finally learned that within me there lay
an invincible summer."
— ALBERT CAMUS

It is a spectacular winter day; just a little under freezing, bright sun chewing at the edges of the snow on the roof and the rocks down by the shore. Far off in the back bay I see the faint outline of a couple people standing on the ice near their snowmobiles. I know exactly what they are up to, and I am gripped by an urge from many years past. Suddenly I have the very silly idea that I should dress up, rummage through the storage shed, haul out some gear, and go ice fishing.

Thankfully, the idea leaves me as quickly as it came. It was a bit scary for a moment, but common sense, plus memories of ice fishing expeditions past, welled up and took control. I'm okay now and steady in my knowledge that ice fishing is one of the most bizarre activities known to humankind.

Why would anyone want to go out onto a frozen lake, labouriously drill holes through a metre of ice, then sit shivering and semi-comatose while jigging a little stick with ice-caked line with a hook and worm on it? Does it not make more sense to put a log on the fire, pour a hot cup of coffee, sit in your favourite armchair by the window, and stare out over the lake?

There are many people out there who obviously have not reached my state of elevated thinking about ice fishing. You see them on lakes everywhere, flapping their arms like penguins trying to build up some body heat. They are truly obsessed.

My late uncle, Len Poling, was one of those. He used to ice fish on Northern Lights Lake west of Thunder Bay. He once experimented with tents that could be held up by forced air. He fashioned a small, clear tent and took it into Northern Lights on a snow tractor. He hauled in a battery, forced air blower, heater, cooking utensils — all the stuff to be comfortable out there on a frozen lake in Arctic weather.

He and a buddy set the thing up and it worked. It was bright and warm in that tent. After a few celebratory drinks the place had really warmed up and they decided it would be a good thing to strip down to their shorts and t-shirts. Unfortunately, they forgot the tent was see through and they attracted a crowd, including a game warden.

Sketch by Zita Poling Moynan.

One of the great mysteries of the outdoors is why people abandon their spacious and warm cottages to sit in a tiny, unheated shack on a frozen lake. I often watch them fighting the elements as I sit sipping coffee in the comfort of my cottage.

As the day progressed, the tent became warmer and warmer, and then hotter and hotter. More drinks were needed to keep cool. Soon, these two ice fishermen realized water was spilling over the tops of their boots. The heat inside the tent was melting the ice and forced them to flee into the freezing cold.

There also is a great ice fishing story from The Canadian Press (CP), the news service where I once worked. The general manager of CP decades ago was Gilles Purcell, a rough and tough leader of men who had lost a leg below the knee during the Second World War. He had an artificial leg named Barney that became famous in CP lore.

GP, as he was fondly and fearfully known, organized an ice fishing trip to Lake Simcoe. The party rented a spacious ice hut with benches lined along a substantial rectangle cut through the ice. Much rum was consumed and at one point GP got up to go outside to relieve himself. He slipped and fell into the fishing hole. During the thrashing about and rescue attempts, Barney shook loose and sank to the bottom. Fortunately the water was shallow and Barney was fished out and reattached.

The rescue of Barney was hailed as a heroic feat, but the indignity of Barney's dunking put a damper on the overall outing.

These are valuable little ice fishing scenes that I tuck away for emergency use. Whenever seized by the crazy urge to don a parka and search out ice fishing gear, I pull them from the back of my mind. Invariably they settle me and chase away the ice fishing urge. They prod me into putting another log on the woodstove, to grab another cup of coffee, and settle into the chair by the window.

— 35 —
SNOWMOBILES

"Snow had fallen, snow on snow, snow on snow,
In the bleak midwinter, Long ago."
— Christina Rossetti, English poet

Another winter pursuit we avoid at Shaman's Rock is the popular sport of snowmobiling. Thousands and thousands of people love to get out on their sleds and explore the winter wonderland. I understand and appreciate that, however snowmobiles and I have a very troubling history. There have been times when I just wanted to pull out my deer rifle, run out to the shed, and shoot one right through the carbs. It is difficult to trace the beginnings of this disdain for snowmobiles, which I might add, is mutual. Snowmobiles I have owned have tried to make me insane, and have even attempted to run me over.

My dislike of these machines is peculiar considering snowmobiles have proven to be a boon to the modern cottager. They have opened up winter country, providing access to cottages once left to hibernate along with the bears. Because of the snowmobiles there now are cottage days spent exploring the land, evenings with a glass of wine beside a roaring woodstove. Fun towing the kids, and all that.

I never witnessed any of the touted joys of snowmobiling. My problems began immediately after acquiring my first used snow machine from a friend who didn't want it anymore. I quickly learned why he wanted to be done with it. It ran real good, but it had a mind of its own and was jinxed.

I brought it to the cottage road, unplowed back then, and pulled it off the back of my truck. I was dressed in light clothing and in a hurry to get to the cottage, which is only one kilometre along the road. I inserted the key, cranked it over, but it wouldn't start. I choked it more. I checked the spark plug wires. I worked feverishly, but I was shivering violently and my teeth were chattering. I kicked the machine and started yelling, just to get warm.

Just as my tantrum was finishing, another snowmobile came up the track from the lake. It was driven by a tall masked mummy who was not showing one square centimetre of bare skin. The mummy walked over to my machine. He lifted a thickly padded right hand, moved it over the handle bars and flicked a thumb across the kill switch. The hand then moved down to key and turned it gently. The snowmobile engine exploded into action, while the mysterious figure mounted his machine and drove off without a word.

That set tone for my relationship with the snowmobile. A few days later it ran out of gas far out on the lake. Then its track hit a rock and went wonky.

Eventually I got a newer, faster machine, which was equally hateful. It sat quite a bit, and the mice made a nest in the carburetor and it burst into flames when I tried to start it.

I got another one but it broke through the ice, thankfully near shore. No one got too wet, but my wife ran screaming off the lake vowing never to get on a snowmobile again. I sold that machine and used the money to buy a used ATV, which proved much easier to start, more reliable, and more useful. I'm able to do some cottage chores with the ATV, something snowmobiles always turned their noses up at.

Snowmobiles I now watch from a distance. At night I see their lights streaking across the lake in front of Shaman's Rock. They are ghosts flying effortlessly across the snow-covered ice, disappearing into the darkness of the forests, following trails that take them to other lakes and other territories.

During the day I can watch them skimming the open water beneath the Dorset bridge. This has become exciting sport. The drivers wind the machines up on the ice in Little Trading Bay and scream full speed until they hit the water. The machines are so powerful now they can stay atop the water indefinitely.

There are tricks to skipping the water. It is best, I'm told, to lean back and keep pressure off the skis. You have to hold the throttle wide open and keep water from splashing into the belt. If the belt begins to slip, you are going to get wet. If the machine is going down, shut off the engine before it submerges.

There are folks who recover machines that don't skip the water too well. They charge healthy fees for recovery, and a big bill to repair a machine that sinks with motor running.

My snowmobile relationships have been unhappy, but thousands of other folks have turned snowmobile travel into a major winter industry. The Ontario Federation of Snowmobile Clubs (OFSC) now boasts approximately 230 local snowmobile clubs. The OFSC has more than 34,000 kilometres of trails across private and public lands, and estimates that annual economic activity generated by its trails is more than $1.2 billion. It estimated that snowmobilers provide $112 million a year in provincial tax revenue.

Exact numbers are unknown but the best guesstimate is that there are 168,000 active snowmobilers in Ontario. The OFSC says that 35 percent of snowmobilers own a cottage.

It's not for me, but it's a terrific sport for people who enjoy winter and either don't want to travel south or can't afford to. There's much to do out there on those many kilometres of snow trails.

— 36 —
SKI TRACKS

"The snow doesn't give a soft white damn whom it touches."
— E.E. CUMMINGS

There is little to disturb the serenity as I snowshoe through the winter woods behind Shaman's Rock. The only sounds are my breathing, and the squishing of my snowshoes on the snow blanket that has been drawn over the carpet of wet leaves.

A chickadee flits from one bare branch to another. He and I seem to be the only living creatures here in a bush that has finally fallen asleep after eight months of frenetic activity since the last snow left in April. The bears have eaten every last morsel they could find in the forest and have crawled into hibernation. The deer appear to have trekked off to thicker winter cover where the snow will be less deep and the cold a bit less brutal.

The turkeys are here somewhere, likely on their roosts in the trees considering what this change of season means to their daily routine. Cold and harder movements as they strut, stop, and scratch the forest floor in the unending pursuit of acorns, beech nuts, seeds, winter hemlock buds, or any plant material or dried berries that will nourish them. With the insects pretty much gone, the pickings are slim.

The walking is not easy. Many smaller trees have been bent over in an ice storm, their top branches now frozen in the snow. I have to skirt patches of these bent trees and think about the snowmobile and cross-country ski trails that will have to be cleared of these obstacles.

Off to my right I hear the sound of a machine. I gather it's Bruce who lives down the highway. He is driving his track groomer through a trail across my property as he heads to the Frost Centre cross-country ski area. Crossing my land saves him driving down the edge of the highway, a convenience for him, and no trouble for me. Anything that helps makes the Frost Centre area an active outdoor destination where people can touch the wilds is good with me.

The Frost Centre trails have been rescued by volunteers called the Ski Friends of the Frost Centre. The trails loop through a beautiful wilderness area across the highway from the locked doors of the Frost Centre. The Friends keep the trail cleared and groomed for paid cross-country skiing.

There are twenty-five kilometres of seven stacked trails named for animals found in the area. The deer trail, for instance, takes skiers through scenic bush country around Three Island Lake for an outing that covers roughly sixteen kilometres return trip. The trails wind across hardwoods ridges, through white pine and hemlock patches, past swamps and outcroppings of the area's famous granite.

One trail passes Dan Lake, and there is a cabin there on the east shore where skiers can rest, get warm, and have a bite to eat to pump up their energy levels. It's a neat shelter in a scenic outdoor setting that makes you feel you are hundreds of kilometres from civilization. There's another one farther out on the moose trail that loops around Three Island Lake. In 2013, skiing the trails cost $13 a day for adults, $9 for half a day, and children under seventeen accompanying an adult don't pay. A season's pass is $70 a person or $140 for a family.

So we have the volunteers of the Friends providing outdoor winter activities on one side of the highway, and Algonquin Highlands Township operating its water and forest trails on the other side. No one knows how long the ski operation will last. The Friends have tried to get local government to take over all the operational, financial, and legal responsibilities for the ski trails. They say their volunteers are getting "burned out."

Meanwhile, the multi-million dollar Frost Centre complex remains empty. Kind of makes you wonder again why someone can't pull it all together, make it a truly active outdoor recreation and education centre, and make a few bucks.

— 37 —
MOONLIGHT

"I believe in God, only I spell it Nature."
— FRANK LLOYD WRIGHT, 1966

I t is time to bank the fire for the night. I stuff the woodstove with logs, dampen the air supply, and hope I get a good slow burn that will allow me to sleep for six hours, perhaps even eight, before I have to get up and add more logs.

I am a champion sleeper, able to sleep through the loudest night sounds and air that becomes sharply cooler as the fire dwindles. This night, however, light is seeping through the windows, urging me to get up to witness an amazing night. I rise and look out at a full moon rising over pine-studded granite cliffs across the lake.

The moon is fat and yellowish. There is no trace of the shrivelled iciness of the Little Spirit Moon of December. I take the increased size and the yellow warmth as a sign that winter is breathing hard in its efforts to stay alive and vigorous, which is good because it is March.

The yellowness disappears as the moon sails above the cliffs, broadcasting white light over the lake and shoreline, a whiteness made whiter by a reflective veil of snow mist. It is almost like daylight; bright enough to see anything moving through the woods. But nothing is moving. The bush is as still as a landscape painting. Even the black shadows of the trees cast down on the moonbeam-sparkled snow are dead still.

It is too still and beautiful a night to sleep. I stay up, feasting long on the winter serenity and reflecting, until I see a rosiness develop at the top edge of the eastern cliff face. The rosiness intensifies and spreads like blood seeping through fresh snow. This is a magnificent winter sunrise that makes you forget the days of snow pounding down and the rock-splitting cold.

It seems impossible that there could be so much peace and calm here when just beyond the sunrise lies a world of chaos. Earthquakes, catastrophic storms, political upheaval.

We are truly blessed here at Shaman's Rock, surrounded by nature's beauty and tranquility. When I compare this place with places and events around the world — and even just down the freeway in the big city — I feel a twinge of guilt. We have this and so many people have nothing.

It's not as if we stole the place, however. We sacrificed much to build this place, and still go without some things to keep it. What I do regret is that the increasing complexities of our society have made this place much more than we ever wanted, or needed. We wanted a simple place in the woods, but the codes and regulations of government, and of course a more affluent society, have made it difficult to have a simple shack on the lake.

Laws controlling building practices and materials, burning, waste handling, shorelines, and a variety of other things have driven the cost of cottaging beyond the reach of more and more people. In many places today the price of a cottage is as much or more than the average house. For most people it is not possible any more to have both.

I think often about what the future holds for this lake country. I think about it a lot because it is the best place on earth. You can travel Europe, the Far East, the Caribbean, wherever. There is beauty, peace and history here like no other place. Maybe that's because every cottager's place is a reflection of themselves and their dreams.

From a physical point of view, nature will take care of cottage country in the future. Water, the source of life, will find ways to get where it is needed. Plants will grow and help cleanse the atmosphere. Scars will heal and eventually fade away. There will always be forests and lakes here, if we work reasonably with nature. And we are trying. As Lorne Heise told me, one of the big changes in cottage life is that "people are very more mindful of the environment."

From a human point of view, who knows what will happen here, especially to Shaman's Rock? Will economic disaster take it from us? Will government someday grab it because the land is needed for roads or airports or some other infrastructure? How does it get passed on and held by people who will appreciate it?

Sketch by Zita Poling Moynan.

When the sun rises at Shaman's Rock, the first thing to give thanks for is nature itself. It is a gift to be cherished and protected.

I don't know the answers, and wonder if finding them really matters. I have heard advice about consulting accountants about future capital gains on cottages, and about consulting lawyers on succession planning and cottage trusts. The fact is there is no way I can guarantee the future of Shaman's Rock.

I can worry and plan until the crows stop cawing. The best I can do is enjoy this place and help others to love and enjoy it. Cottages are the dreams of a special type of people. They pass away with the people who have them, and are picked up again by people who yearn to experience them.

The best plan is to stay here, forever. We both want our ashes spread here because this is where we have been closest to being our real selves. We belong here as part of nature. No matter what name is on the deed, no matter how many years or circumstances pass, we will be a part of this. No one owns the land forever, but it is ours forever if we become part of it.

I gaze out at the pink dawn, and I feel a tightening ache from the top of my stomach to bottom of my throat. This place is achingly beautiful. It has made me realize what it means to truly love something. It has made me better understand the Native American view of the land. Survey stakes and deeds are the inventions of men; much the same as are calendar dates that mark the beginnings of spring, summer, autumn, and winter. Nature owns the land and we are a part of nature.

I picture this place as I first saw it, an ancient granite outcropping thrust out among the trees. On it stands a shaman — not the mystical medicine man of books and films, but a simple man who asks simple questions for which there are no simple answers. In the end, he lifts his face to the brightening sky, outstretches his arms to welcome the rising sun, and chants:

> Gchi miigwech gzhemnidoo
> Kina gegoo emiizhyang
> Miinwa ngoding gii-giizhaak
> Giizis gii binaabia
> Gchi miigwech gii miizhyang
> Iw sa bimaadziwin

It is a small prayer thanking his Great Spirit for everything he receives: thanks for another day, thanks for another rising sun, and thanks for life itself. His mind cannot fully comprehend the concept of a Great Spirit, or to truly know whether one exists. That is just another question for which there is no simple answer. What he does know, does comprehend, and does believe in, is nature around him.

Dawn is well established, and it is time to catch some sleep. The sun has reached the cottage metal roof as I climb the stairs to my bed. Before I nod off under the duvet, I hear that first welcome sound of spring. *Plink. Plink.*

One cycle ends, another begins.

SUGGESTED READING

Echoes of the Past
Ed Devitt and Nila Reynolds
Privately Printed, 1965

The Gilmour Tramway: A Lumber Baron's Desperate Scheme
Gary Long
Fox Meadow Creations, 2008

The Global Forest
Diana Beresford-Kroeger
Viking Press, 2010

Last Child in the Woods: Saving Our Children from Nature-Deficit Disorder
Richard Louv
Algonquin Books, 2005

A Life in the Bush: Lessons from My Father
Roy MacGregor
Penguin Books Canada, 2000

A Life in the Country
Bruce Hutchison
Douglas & McIntyre, 1988

Mosquito: The Story of Man's Deadliest Foe
Andrew Spielman, Sc.D., and Michael D'Antonio
Hyperion, 2002

Tom Thomson: The Life and Mysterious Death of the Famous Canadian Painter
Jim Poling Sr.
Altitude Publishing, 2003

ABOUT THE AUTHOR

Jim Poling Sr. is the author of ten books, including *Waking Nanabijou* and *Smoke Signals: The Native Takeback of North America's Tobacco Industry*. His magazine work has appeared in *Cottage Life*, *Ontario Out of Doors*, and *Readers' Digest*. His residence is in Barrie, Ontario, but he spends more than half his time, summer and winter, at his cottage, Shaman's Rock on St. Nora Lake just south of Dorset.

INDEX

ALSO BY JIM POLING, SR.

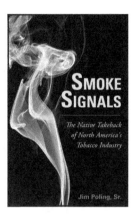

Smoke Signals
The Native Takeback of North America's Tobacco Industry
9781459706408
$24.99

When Europeans discovered tobacco among Amerindians in the New World, it became a long-sought panacea of panaceas, the critical ingredient in enemas, ointments, syrups, and powders employed to treat everything from syphilis to cancer. Almost five centuries passed before medical researchers concluded that tobacco is unhealthy and can cause cancer.

Smoke Signals follows tobacco from its origins in South America's Andes through its checkered history as a "miracle cure," powerful addictive and poison, friend of government revenue departments, and enemy of law enforcement directed at contraband and tax diversion. Author Jim Poling, Sr., traces tobacco's sacredness among Natives, notably how the modern substance has changed Native lives, sometimes for the good, often for the bad, explores how the coffers of governments, now so dependent on tobacco revenue, will be affected if the plant's commercial use is eliminated, and examines how Native traditions, including tobacco as a holy herb, might survive in modern society and strengthen Natives.

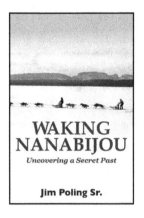

Waking Nanabijou
Uncovering a Secret Past
9781550027570
$26.99

A woman from Northern Ontario is buried; her earthly papers reveal a mystery. Veteran Canadian journalist Jim Poling took on the most important assignment of his career. Just who was his mother? Why did she take a lifelong secret to her grave?

In his search for clues throughout his childhood years in Northern Ontario, the author goes to Chapleau, the railway town where the people he believed were his ancestors played out their roles in building the railway. It ends in the Prairie village of Innisfree, Alberta, home to Joe LaRose, convicted horse thief and father of a girl destined for trouble.

A search that began in anger at his mother's secrecy concludes with an understanding of her actions. In the process, he explores the place of families within Canadian society and reveals the shameful ongoing discrimination against Native Peoples and the abusive treatment of illegitimacy. Throughout, glimpses of working life in newsrooms add insider perspectives on the "handling" of our daily news.

www.dundurn.com

VISIT US AT
Dundurn.com
Definingcanada.ca
@dundurnpress
Facebook.com/dundurnpress